Return to
the Place I
Never Left

Return to the Place I Never Left

Tobias Schiff

Translated by Dani James

WAYNE STATE UNIVERSITY PRESS
DETROIT

ISBN 9780814351628 (paperback)
ISBN 9780814352434 (hardcover)
ISBN 9780814351635 (ebook)

Library of Congress Control Number: 2024933491

Cover art © Envato. Cover design by Elke Barter.

Publication of this book was made possible through the generosity of the Bertha M. and Hyman Herman Endowed Memorial Fund.

Wayne State University Press rests on Waawiyaataanong, also referred to as Detroit, the ancestral and contemporary homeland of the Three Fires Confederacy. These sovereign lands were granted by the Ojibwe, Odawa, Potawatomi, and Wyandot Nations, in 1807, through the Treaty of Detroit. Wayne State University Press affirms Indigenous sovereignty and honors all tribes with a connection to Detroit. With our Native neighbors, the press works to advance educational equity and promote a better future for the earth and all people.

Wayne State University Press
Leonard N. Simons Building
4809 Woodward Avenue
Detroit, Michigan 48201-1309

Visit us online at wsupress.wayne.edu.

Contents

Translator's Preface

The first time I read *Return to the Place I Never Left*, originally titled *Terug op de plaats die ik nooit heb verlaten*, its title rang true and clear. Here is the story of a man, Tobias (Toshek) Schiff, who survived eight nazi camps. Concentration camps. Places of terror, abuse, and murder. Places where memories—rather, remembrances—are formed that don't, can't leave a person. In the years since, I've continued to return to the book.

A memoir written in verse, its departure from convention and conformity was apparent as soon as I looked at its pages. Words were not neatly spread out from the left margin to the right but clustered in rhythmic bunches forming sentences that revealed the memories of a man who experienced pain, extensive and deep. Toshek's stories outlined a period of his life filled with death and despair. His words read like truths that landed with the weight of a boulder. There were no traditional sentences, only names were capitalized and punctuation was rare, resulting in a book that read like a stream of consciousness. Reading his memoir, becoming familiar with his long journey through the death camps, seeing his tenacity while broken, beaten, and starved, and learning what enabled him and others to cling to the last shred of life while surrounded by death cracked me open. His voice, clear even when toggling between remembrance, confession, and confusion, drew me in, bringing me back to reread his work, and again.

Toshek was born in Poland to Jewish parents in 1925. He grew up in Antwerp, Belgium, where he spoke Yiddish at home. His knowledge of the language, with its German and Polish influences, would prove lifesaving for him after the nazis invaded. When he was seventeen years old, his sister disappeared among a string of violent raids and laws targeting Jewish people, sparking an urgent escape. Toshek and his parents attempted to flee the country but were captured and deported. Toshek spent the next four years imprisoned in concentration camps doing forced labor, in a near-constant state of starvation, encircled by death. He survived. His mother, father, and sister did not.

Toshek's survival marked the beginning of a life spent simultaneously trying to remember and forget, a life spent carrying—and passing on—harrowing memories and deeply rooted trauma. He committed to sharing his story to raise awareness to prevent genocides from recurring, giving testimonies in schools and documentaries, culminating in the Flemish version of the written work you now hold in your hands. Through sharing his story, he was able to provide a firsthand account of his experience. Through sharing his story, he was also able to give voice to the experiences of his mother, father, sister, friends, relatives, and community members who were murdered during the Holocaust.

The Holocaust refers to the deliberately planned systematic and state-sponsored persecution and murder of approximately six million Jewish people and millions of others, including Romani people, members of the LGBTQ+ community, people with mental illnesses, political dissidents, Jehovah's Witnesses, and more by nazi Germany and its collaborators during World War II. It is one of the most horrific events in modern history, the outcome of letting hatred, discrimination, and racism fester. The nazis persecuted anyone they considered a threat to the purity of the so-called aryan race, the fabricated, ultra-white group of Europeans they considered the master race. World War II took place between 1939 and 1945, but anti-semitism raged in Europe and other parts of the world long before then. In the late nineteenth and early twentieth centuries, vicious waves of violence against Jewish populations in Russia erupted. Dubbed pogroms, these were organized attacks. During a pogrom, a mob of civilians (or authorities) frenzied through an area, targeting people who were ethnically or religiously underrepresented, resulting in physical violence, destruction of property, and death. These attacks caused millions of Jewish people to flee the region to countries across the world. They searched for new homes and planted roots in places that included Belgium, where Toshek's family ended up, and Germany.

In the aftermath of World War I and during the Great Depression, Germany's economy was broken, leading to widespread poverty, unemployment, and social unrest. Desolate conditions contributed to the rise of Adolf Hitler and his political party, the nazis, in the early 1930s. Shortly after they gained power in 1933, the first restrictive laws against Jewish people were implemented. These laws marked the beginning of the state-sponsored persecution of Jews in Germany. Like all discriminatory laws, this had profoundly detrimental effects.

It started with the dismissal of Jewish civil servants. From one day to the next, they were jobless, no longer allowed to perform their professions. It continued with laws that included the Law for the Protection of German Blood and German Honor, which prohibited marriages between Jewish and non-Jewish people; the Reich Citizenship Law, which stripped Jewish Germans of their citizenship; laws that limited participation in schools and universities; and laws that restricted Jewish participation in society, effectively marginalizing the community.

Then came the identification laws. In 1938, the Law on the Alteration of Family and Personal Names required all Jewish people whose name did not reflect their Jewish heritage to add a middle name to their identification documents. Women were forced to adopt the middle name *Sara*, men the middle name *Israel*. Later that year, the identity documents of Jewish people were stamped with a glaring letter *J*, for *Jude* (Jew). Soon after, the Jewish population was forced to wear a yellow Star of David on their clothing, making it easier for nazis to identify and target them. This was one of many actions taken to stigmatize Jewish people and isolate them further from the rest of the population. The Star of David, a symbol of the Jewish religion, became a marker, a branding, stitched onto people's clothes so they could easily be picked out in a crowd and publicly humiliated, the star a flaming bull's-eye. Indeed, in the years that followed, people wearing the Jewish badge were brutally beaten, segregated into ghettos, subjected to forced labor, and deported to concentration camps and incarceration sites. In 1941, nazis launched what they called the Final Solution, the mass murder of European Jews. They leveraged mass shootings and mobile gas vans to kill Jewish communities at scale. They built extermination camps, also known as death camps or killing centers, where large gas chambers increased the number of people murdered each day. According to the United States Holocaust Museum, "at the height of the deportations, an average of 6,000 Jews were gassed each day at the Auschwitz II (Birkenau) killing center." This is one of the camps Toshek survived. The nazis and their collaborators decimated Europe's Jewish population. By 1945, six million Jewish people and millions of others were dead.

Like Toshek, my grandparents, too, were Holocaust survivors. They were teenagers when the war broke out, forcing them to separate from their families and into hiding. They survived by doing just that. Hiding. Living clandestinely in hospitals, hiding between secret walls, concealing their identities. They were alone, in places and households where no one knew exactly what happened behind closed doors. It shaped the rest of their lives, and therefore the lives of their children, grandchildren, and generations to follow. By the time *Return to the Place I Never Left* entered my home by way of Toshek's daughter, a close friend of my mother's, I'd heard testimonies directly from relatives who survived in different ways. My grandfather survived a raid in a German hospital by hiding among dead bodies in a morgue. My grandmother hid in a family's home and served as their maid. False identification documents were part of the plan to keep them safe. (I remember seeing these documents when I was younger. Here was my grandmother, dark-haired with thick glasses, the name on one document the one she was born with, Rosa Joanna Weizer. Above her photo, a stamp blaring *JOOD—JUIF* in red ink. A Star of David stamped next to her name. In another document, the one created for survival, her hair was lighter, her glasses were gone. Her name was changed to Rosa Jeanne Fairon, a name that hid her heritage.) My uncle's grandmother was thrown into a mass grave in a concentration camp. There she lay until a rat bit her forehead, startling her awake. She waited until the sky darkened to crawl out of the pit of dead bodies. These narratives were my family's history, defining moments that shaped their lives, and therefore mine.

While Toshek's memoir explores a subject my family history is entrenched in, his work is unique in that it approaches a deeply painful topic in an unexpected and accessible way. The language is direct and conversational, the sentences succinct and present. This is a book with space on the pages that leaves room for air, room to contemplate its heavy, necessary subject matter, allowing the reader to become a witness alongside Toshek, getting to know his thoughts, absorbing scenes he witnessed and the confronting moments where he struggles to make sense of things, and tries to remember instances he no longer sees clearly.

Return to the Place I Never Left's content—grounded in oral history—drives its form, providing a swiftly paced, visual retelling of Toshek's life that remains with the reader long after finishing the last page. This puts his work in the company of contemporary memoirs that weave together the narrative of the writer's life through poetic images, like Jacqueline Woodson's *Brown Girl Dreaming*, and those that incorporate political vision through memoiristic expression, like *Dead Weight* by Randall Horton. Similar to Elie Wiesel, who recounted his survival as a teenager in Auschwitz-Birkenau in *Night*, Toshek describes chilling scenes recalled from his lived experiences, bringing the reader into a world within the one we know, where breadcrumbs save a person's life and an infected wound attracting flies becomes a source of hope. Toshek writes of the time he's able to convince an SS officer to let him sleep on a table for a few hours:

> below the stage people screamed
> they were sick
> they were dying
> they urinated and defecated in place
> if someone stood up he stepped on his neighbor
> and I lay there on that table
> a royal bed
> eating crumbs

In just a few lines, he illustrates a horrific time in a terrible place that meant the end of life for most who were in that same space at that same time. He also showcases the hierarchies that were able to—however briefly—exist among prisoners.

Insults and commands were ever-present in the concentration camps. Screamed at prisoners by the SS guards surrounding them. *Ihr dreckige schweine.* Toshek presents these in their original language, enabling the orders to echo in the reader's mind in German. The choice to depart from traditional sentence structure enables him to maintain the fluidity of an oral text, with no period to mark the end of the sentence, just like there is no end to his experience, no way to render it complete. This is exemplified when he shares a postwar conversation:

someone once asked
'have you ever tried
to remove that number on your arm?'
I said
'who can remove it
from my head?'

After publication, *Return to the Place I Never Left* became required reading for high school students in Flanders for several years. It was later translated into French. I am honored to have translated the first English version, which you are holding in your hands. In my translation, I kept Toshek's stylistic approaches, occasionally adding a line break to add a pause or dashes to provide clarification. I preserved the text in other languages, at times adding additional translations. Run-on chapters were restructured into vignettes to enable readers to reflect on the story at their own pace. In the original text, nazis are often referred to as "SS'ers" which stands for members of the Schutzstaffel (SS), the guards of the nazi regime. In the decades since the war, the term is not as recognizable anymore, and many use the umbrella term "nazis" to represent the regime's people in various roles during the Holocaust. For this reason, I use the terms "nazis" and "SS guard" or "SS officer" interchangeably throughout the translated text. I intentionally lowercase the word "nazis" to align with Toshek's capitalization style and because of my conviction that the term, the regime, and the rhetoric they represent should not be capitalized.

Since the initial publication of *Return to the Place I Never Left* three decades ago, genocides have persisted. Atrocities committed against people for their identity and the communities they're born into persist. Patterns of inequity persist. People continue to have to hide to survive. History reaches back and repeats what has come before in a different part of the world, targeting different people. In *Survivor: The Triumph of an Ordinary Man in the Khmer Rouge Genocide*, Chum Mey reveals he was held at the infamous S-21/Tuol Sleng prison in the late 1970s. He was shackled. He was tortured, beaten, and starved. Any day, at any moment, he could die. Of the estimated 15,000 prisoners detained at Tuol Sleng, 12 survived. In *Left to Tell: Discovering God Amidst the Rwandan Holocaust*, Immaculée Ilibagiza describes how, in 1994, she and seven other women spent three months in a tiny bathroom, hiding from Hutu militias intent on eradicating people of her Tutsi heritage. During the Rwandan genocide, an estimated 800,000 to 1 million people were murdered in 100 days. Immaculée survived. Her mother, father, and brother did not. In documenting their stories, Toshek, Chum, and Immaculée became part of an important community of survivors who revealed some of their most horrifying experiences. These authors bear witness, provide historical records, and ensure the atrocities they observed are not forgotten. They provide evidence of the genocide, countering denial theories and revisionist narratives aimed at distorting or minimizing historical facts.

In an age of rampant disinformation, division, and people engaging with their communities in physical and virtual bubbles, it appears the world has become more polarized, people have become more disconnected from one another, and us-versus-them narratives that ignore our collectiveness as human beings thrive. There is little room for nuanced dialogue. Complex issues are memeified and grossly oversimplified. The ongoing global refugee crisis, wars and armed conflicts, and resurgence of overt anti-semitism and islamophobia remind us that books examining the impact of racism, discrimination, and forced displacement remain necessary. These are universal experiences, affecting not just the people who survive them but their children, and those yet to be born. In addition to providing educational context, memoirs help humanize those targeted in genocides. They put a name, a face, a person to the statistic. They give insight into individuals, their lives, what they care about, their resilience, and their strength. It's challenging to discount someone once they share their personal story. It's hard to hold on to preconceived notions about an individual after dialogue with them and becoming aware of shared beliefs, interests, experiences, or favorite meals. Sharing experiences with one another via authentic forms of storytelling can be a powerful tool to challenge dehumanizing narratives.

Most Holocaust survivors are no longer alive. Toshek is no longer alive. My grandparents are no longer alive. This translation is my way to ensure the stories and people of this generation are not forgotten. Like Toshek, I hope sharing his story will raise awareness of the dangerous impact of unchecked hatred and prejudice, and help prevent future genocides. I hope that you'll find reading this book meaningful. Perhaps you'll reread it from time to time. Above all, I hope this serves as a reminder that to be human is to be part of a collective, to be alive is a gift.

Dani James

Return to the Place I Never Left

A Note from the Original Publisher

In 1988, filmmaker Jean-Marc Turine conducted a series of conversations with Tobias Schiff as preparation for a film. The film was recorded on December 22 of that same year and is titled *Monsieur S*. It lasted twenty-six minutes, a restriction placed by the TV channel. But how was it possible to, in such a short time frame, report on the full breadth of the nazi system, with its vicious implementation? Was such a pared-down version not an injustice to the thirty-three months Schiff spent imprisoned, fourteen of which were spent in Auschwitz? Was the essential not excluded? Turine wanted to dedicate the time needed to allow viewers to *feel* what that deportation was like, but couldn't go over twenty-six minutes. For this reason, he transcribed and published every conversation he had with Schiff. The transcribed text was edited by Hilde Desmet and became the basis of this book. In a series of conversations and meetings with Schiff in Brussels, we kneaded and fleshed out those texts to their current literary expressiveness.

The stories revealed here are true. They are irrefutably established. It is, however, possible that, here or there, a date is not exact. Even a memory that's been trained for fifty years to remember can show signs of weakness.

While sharing his story, Schiff repeated commands shouted by the SS in German before translating them. I kept these expressions in German because I wanted to preserve the rhythm of Schiff's way of thinking and manner of speaking. It was as if that language helped him recall memories, helped him see the executioners, see his friends again. It brought him right back to Breendonk, Dora, Auschwitz. It enabled him to share feelings and experiences that are hard to verbalize and impossible to forget.

Hugo Franssen

to my wife
who with love and self-hate
for over twenty-five years
has shared and tolerated
the burden of my experience

to all who did not return

to my father Moshe Schiff
murdered by the German Schutzstaffel
and their accomplices
in the gas chambers
of Auschwitz-Birkenau
on Friday January 21 1944
he was 46 years old

to my mother Regina Templer-Schiff
murdered by the German Schutzstaffel
and their accomplices
in the gas chambers
of Auschwitz-Birkenau
early in September of 1942
she was 40 years old

to my sister Lunia Schiff
murdered by the German Schutzstaffel
and their accomplices
in the gas chambers
of Auschwitz-Birkenau
on October 15 1942
she was 19 years old

and
to my children
Anny
Maurice
Lunia
Dominique
to Isabelle my last little one
and all my grandchildren

to my aunt Toni
and my uncle Maurice
and my 'little sister' Estelle

Silence slowly prevails and then, from my bunk on the top row, I see and hear old Kuhn praying aloud, beret on his head, swaying backwards and forwards violently. Kuhn is thanking God because he hasn't been chosen. Kuhn is out of his mind. Does he not see, in the bunk next to him Beppo, who is 20 years old and going to the gas chamber the day after tomorrow? Beppo knows it and lies there staring at the light, not saying anything, not even thinking anymore. Does Kuhn not understand that next time it will be his turn? That what has happened today is an abomination, which no propitiatory prayer, no pardon, no apology—nothing in the power of man—can ever wipe clean again? If I was God, I would spit at Kuhn's prayer.

—Primo Levi, *If This Is a Man*

Whoever listens to a witness, becomes a witness.

—Elie Wiesel

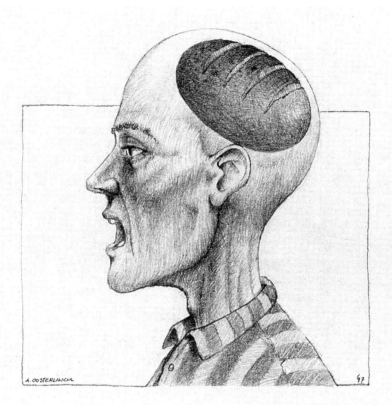

A. OOSTERLINCK   97

1

mother

I try to understand

I've been trying for 50 years
thinking thinking
sometimes
without realizing that I'm thinking
that I'm asking myself questions
I ask and stop ask and stop ask and stop
I want to know
what happened?
how did it happen?
always the same same same
                              questions

it doesn't let me go
they don't let me go
never

where did they go?
did they ever exist?
yes there are memories and
          if I don't write them down
          they never existed
          if I don't read my own words or don't talk about it
          they disappear
          the day I die they die
          again
          this time we'll disappear together

I owe it to them
I had a father a mother like everyone else
I had a sister
father was 46
mother 39
Lunia was about to turn 19 in a few days
there is no consolation
there will never be
they were murdered
          poisoned by gas
          industrial murder

there is no solace there is no grave
if I don't write about them
they never existed
grandmothers grandfathers uncles aunts nieces nephews
more than 100 people
        more than 100 names
                more than 100 faces
all gone all dead
ghosts ghosts

if I don't write about them they are ghosts
if I don't write about them they never existed

they did exist
they were here
I knew them I saw them I hugged them
I'm writing it down
so they are here
so they can live
yes they're here
they were here

I can see them
see them all
        all the time
        see all of our times
until I remember

they disappeared
went up in smoke
their darkened ash blurs my mind
each time I remember

but right now
my eyes are closed and
in front of me they are here and
this time they will stay
they will
stay

where did they go?

why did they go?
there is no solace there is no grave

why did I survive?
me? out of all people
what about those who were better than me?
what about the babies?
little toddlers with tiny fingers and toes
how am I still here? of all people
there is no consolation
there is no grave
as if they never existed
as if they were never really here

if I write about them
they live
they're alive here with me now
through my pen I press them into the paper
make them exist again
each drop of ink a nose hand cheek mother father sister
each memory a life reinstated
they are here

it's 1:00 am
Wednesday March 12 1997
55 years have passed
and they remain gone
there is no way to bring them back
no way to fill the empty left behind
no way to forget they were once here

I was born in 1925 in Tarnów in Poland

my sister Lunia was born in 1923
her official name was Bajla Batja
our father came from Poland to Belgium in 1926
my mother my sister and me we followed him in 1928
at home Yiddish was the language that rolled off our tongues
we lived in the Uitbreidingstraat 578 in Berchem in Antwerp
father worked as a diamond cleaver
sawing each diamond very precisely
tapping it gently
blading through the rough to reveal
a sparkle that wasn't there before

when the Germans invaded in 1940

I was 18 years old
we fled to France
but the French sent us back to Antwerp
my parents thought we could sit tight and wait
for the war to end
everyone else we knew
hoped for the same

then came the first anti-Jewish laws

new IDs were delivered that read
jude
        Jew in German
I believe it was December 1941
we wore the Star of David
we were no longer allowed to go to school
we were no longer allowed to walk in the park
then came the nightly curfew
the law that forbade Jewish people to leave their houses
between 7:00 pm and 7:00 am
we were not allowed in the street during those hours
so we rushed home every evening
running to lock ourselves in

Lunia was arrested on Wednesday July 22 in 1942[1]
the evening before Tisha B'Av
the remembrance of the destruction of the Holy Temple in Jerusalem
Lunia glittered with energy she worked hard
my big sister knew about things and always wanted to learn more
she had a smile that warmed and a wave to her hair
she had plans for her future

I adored my sister
but as a teenager my big sister was very close with her friends and
I wasn't part of their circle
I'll never get over the fact that I didn't know her better
and that on Wednesday July 22
everything stopped

that Wednesday Lunia left with a friend
and didn't return home by 7:00 pm
my parents worried but couldn't notify the authorities
we weren't allowed to have a phone anymore
we didn't know what to think
my parents clutched at the hope
that Lunia accompanied her friend home
and perhaps once there she'd noticed it was too late
to get home before curfew

so we waited the night long and tense

the next morning
the father of Lunia's friend came
he asked if his daughter spent the night with us

later that day we heard about the raid

     the first raid in Belgium
     the German *feldgendarmerie* burst in and around the stations at
     Antwerpen-Centraal Brussel-Noord and Brussel-Zuid
     like a flood they spilled into trains trams cars into the street
     arresting
     every
     single
     Jewish person
Lunia and her friend were captured in the Pelikaanstraat
near the station in Antwerp
we never saw them again

after the war I learned

that Lunia and other prisoners were locked up
at Breendonk and from there transferred to
the Dossinkazerne in Mechelen
from there she was deported

she was part of convoy number 7
which left on Tuesday September 1 1942
her number was 64
convoy number 7 had 1,000 prisoners
it arrived at Auschwitz 2 days later

after the war I met someone who was with my sister at Auschwitz
she survived there for a few weeks
before being gassed

in March 1997 I found her name and the date of her death
in the Auschwitz *sterbebücher*
       October 15 1942
       3 days before her 19th birthday
seeing her in these death books
led to many nights without sleep

deportation convoys received absolute priority

everything yielded to let them pass
even the war provision for the Eastern front made way for
the deportations to Auschwitz and Treblinka
a decision made by nazi leaders and German officials
during the Wannsee conference with the war in full swing

when the Germans got stuck by the Russian front
the speeding up of deportations became the priority
the youngest deportee in Belgium was 34 days old
the oldest was 93

sometime after Lunia's arrest

scammers rang our doorbell
they asked for money to get Lunia home
said we could pay for her freedom
they claimed it was possible to get her back from Breendonk
                              to bring her back to safety

sharpeyed they preyed
on families
on people gripped with fear

we tried to escape to Switzerland

passeurs could help us cross the demarcation line in France
and later the Swiss border
father paid 30,000 francs per person
for mother for him and for me

we left Antwerp on Monday August 10 1942
we were instructed to go to the Koningin Astridplein
in the center of Antwerp between the station and zoo at 10:00 am and
stand by one of the brown marble benches
we had fake IDs
someone would give us an agreed-upon signal to follow
him or her to the train headed to Brussels
and indeed
this is how it happened

that morning before we left our house
my mother used a small pair of scissors to
cut the Star of David from our jackets
she wore her amber-colored coat on the train and
the woman seated across from us stared at her
a hard unrelenting stare
mother looked away and back
the woman stared into her chest
mother's hand gripped tight around mine
she glanced down and realized the imprint of the star was still
visible on her coat
she placed her purse in front of her breast
kept it there and thanked the woman with her eyes
this detail I won't forget

we arrived at the Gare du Nord in Paris

and from there took a bus to Gare de Lyon
the 2 *passeurs* never stood next to us
they got in before or after us and
sat far from us

that evening we took a train
we were all spread out
a group of 14 people running from or for our lives
among us were our neighbors who were friends of my parents
and their 2-year-old daughter
at midnight we arrived in a small city in the region of Orleans

we walked together with our friends
I carried their baby girl on my shoulders
I was 17
we followed the 2 *passeurs*
in the distance we heard dogs bark
we thought there were farms nearby
and that the dogs had smelled us
so we ran
straight through fields and forests

we heard the dogs around 3:00 am

they were closer
their barks curled around us
suddenly lights crisscrossed our bodies
large flashlights lit us up
'halt! stehen bleiben!'
4 or 5 men stood with their machine guns aimed at us
police dogs by their sides
it was the German *feldgendarmerie*

the 2 *passeurs* had disappeared
      did they sell us out?
      were they able to escape because they knew the area?
      did they have a deal with the Germans?
I don't know
all I know is that they weren't chased after

the officers asked for our IDs
'das sind falsche pässe
      ihr seid alle juden ihr versucht zu fliehen'
'those are fake IDs
      you are Jews trying to flee'
they tore our papers
threw the shreds on the ground

we were brought to a small castle
and locked away in a large hall with beautiful high ceilings
I remember Benzion Gottlob
my father's friend
he was against the wall crying
body shaking
'du kimmt men nicht mehr lebendig heroïs'
'we will never leave here alive'
over and over again he said
'das is di ende
noechdem ist gar nicht'
'this is the end
after this there is nothing'

there were 1,000 deportees in our convoy

8 returned
>   6 Frenchmen
>   mister Gottlob
>   and me

the next morning we were brought to a courtyard
that's where it started
from that moment I made sure to always be first
to stand in the first row

I asked the German officer
'was wird mit uns passieren?'
'what will happen to us?'
'ihr werdet alle erschossen'
'you will all be shot to death'
he said it so nonchalantly
as if it were an invitation to coffee
as if he told me the time
as if he said it was a clear-skied day
we were ordered to get into Citroëns and
brought to the prison in Bourges

I must specify that from that moment on we were
under the jurisdiction of the French police
I must also tell you that we had hidden our valuables
under the heels of our right foot
father had $50 mother $30 and I $20
some people had diamonds like mister Gottlob

I was interrogated first
in a square hall with a large table in the back
behind the table sat an officer of the Gestapo and a lady
a young blonde woman
the officer asked me my name and occupation
'diamantencleaver'
'diamond cleaver'
'ah diamantenschwindler!'
'ah a diamond swindler!'

'*uhm . . . diamantencleaver*'
'*wo sind deine diamanten?*'
'where are your diamonds?'
he seemed cheerful
I explained that the cleaver does not own
the diamonds he works on
just like a goldsmith doesn't own
the gold he shapes

he pretended to believe my story
'*das hast du wirklich schön erzählt*'
'you've truly explained this well'
then his tone turned sharp and dry
'*wo sind deine diamanten?*'
'*ich habe keine diamanten*'
'I don't have any diamonds'
'*gib mir deine jacke*'
'give me your jacket'
he ruffled through my jacket
found nothing
threw it back to me and said
'*hast du wirklich keine diamanten?*'
'you really don't have any diamonds?'
'no'
'*wir haben einen holländischen juden geschnappt
und 100,000 gulden in seinen shuh gefunden*'
'we arrested a Jew from Holland
and found 100,000 guldens in his shoe'[2]
'I have nothing'
'*wenn ich etwas finde wirst du erschossen*'
'if I find anything you will be shot to death
give me your shoe'
I took off my left shoe

the woman next to the officer placed a box with tools on the table
with a large screwdriver the officer loosened my sole
then tore it off with 2 large pliers
he found nothing and threw the shoe at me

before he had the chance to ask
I bent down to take my right shoe off
but he spoke
said
'ist schon gut'
'it's fine'

later that day when we were all locked together in a cell
they laughed at my gaping shoe
I discovered the Gestapo officer hadn't asked anyone else
about shoes
or about diamonds

the money in our shoes saved the lives of father and me later in Trzebinia
father traded it for some bread butter and sugar
in Trzebinia half a bread was worth about 10 rations
but that is a story for later

how does one describe hunger?

it's nearly impossible
it started in Bourges
I remember that as a child I didn't like fat
I just couldn't swallow it
        couldn't be made to swallow it
in the prison of Bourges we got
bread in the morning and a soup that looked like machine oil at noon
        I wouldn't eat it
        couldn't stand the smell
        pinched my nostrils closed
        it made me gag

the next day I
lifted my fingers from my nose

the third day I pushed
the layer of fat that topped the soup to the side
took a spoon and a few sips
my stomach gnawed at its own center

the fourth day
I ate obediently
like everyone else

we spent 10 days in 1 prison cell in Bourges

the guard delivered food through a slot in the door
we were just like the other prisoners
we never left the space they'd locked us into
the guards were French

let me think for a moment
yes we were all together
mother was there
I see her again yes
wait
I'm not completely sure

on Friday August 21 they loaded us on a train to Pithiviers

they put us in handcuffs
which I was able to remove
by contorting my hands
to make them as small as possible

the train moved slow
so slow I could've jumped off
but at the time there didn't seem to be a reason to escape
father and mother were on the train with me too
we thought only of staying together

we stayed in Pithiviers for 1 or 2 nights
it was there I saw fleas for the first time
we sat and slept on straw
it was warm and they jumped
in frantic little leaps

then we were brought to the French deportation departure point
an area named Drancy near Paris
we arrived there on Saturday
August 22 or Sunday August 23
they cut our hair off
I remember how the little girl
who lived next door to us laughed and pointed at me
her mother barely recognized me
because I'd lost my curls

on Friday August 28

we were placed on transport number 25
direction Auschwitz

right before our departure the French gendarmes
took all of our belongings
money watches bracelets gold necklaces rings
they took my pocket watch
a gendarme saw the chain and without a word
tore the watch loose
he glanced at it and put it in his pocket
'ça tu n'as plus besoin'
'this you don't need anymore'

they did the work of the nazis
for the nazis
they weren't forced to do it
but they did
they collaborated
made themselves rich
walked through thousands of captives
patting tearing grabbing
taking all that they could

transport number 25 of Friday August 29 1942

was made up of 1,000 deportees
about 280 children
220 women
and 500 men
and
like I mentioned
only 8 of them returned

we sat in closed wagons meant to transport cattle

it was searing hot
everyone got half a bread and a small bottle of water
so small that with the heat
it was finished fast
in the corner an empty bucket operated as toilet
it ran over on the first night

the transport lasted 3 days and 3 nights

women small children
screaming crying sh shh shhh-ing
at the end of the third day the train stopped
in a small station at Koźle in Silesia
it was dark
SS officers* pulled open the wagon doors
searchlights blistered our view
when our eyes adjusted
we saw them

I remember the SS commander
who oversaw the scene
he was clearly in charge
straight backed with his chin high in the air
he wore a white jacket
a dog on a leash on one hand
and in his other hand
a whip

the nazis shouted
'männer raus! frauen und kinder bleiben!'
'men out! women and children stay!'
I wanted to stay with mother
we said goodbye to father
the SS officers climbed into the wagons
to ensure their orders were followed
one of them asked me how old I was
'17 years old'
'raus!'
'out!'

---

* The Schutzstaffel (SS) started out in 1925 as Adolf Hitler's personal bodyguards and grew to become the nazi regime's most powerful paramilitary organization. From 1929 to 1945, the SS was the agency of security, surveillance, brutality, and terror within Germany and German-occupied Europe. The SS was comprised of different units responsible for combat, enforcing the racial policy of nazi Germany, and running the concentration camps. Additional branches of the SS included the Gestapo (secret police) and the Sicherheitsdienst (surveillance and security service). They eliminated nazi opposition, policed people to ensure commitment to nazi ideology, provided domestic and foreign intelligence, and rounded up Jewish people to deport to concentration camps.—Trans.

today I have a document that proves
black ink on white paper
that the SS had received the order to remove men
between the ages of 18 to 45 from the train
— first selection —
that means that when I said
'17'
the SS officer either didn't listen
or ignored the order
that was the first time I got lucky
he knew what would happen to the people
who stayed on the train

I saw mother get out of the wagon

while the SS grouped the men together
days without anything to drink left us all parched
she held a small jar
she was looking for water
the SS commander noticed her and
slashed her in the face with his whip
'rein!'
'get in!'

my last image of her
face bloody
climbing back
into the wagon

she was born in Tarnów in 1902
she was the daughter of Pinkas Templer
she had 7 brothers and sisters
she was dedicated to her children
knitted us sweaters
patched our socks
she ran the house our entire family
and made it lively
she spoiled me
she was proud of her children
I always thought that maybe she was a bit disappointed
in being the wife of a cleaver
though she never said it

mother always looked elegant
she handmade her own dresses
long sometimes slinky
with well-placed buttons
on Tuesday September 1 1942
her life ended
she was 40

we ended up in Sakrau

not far from Auschwitz
we had to march for multiple hours
there were about 300 of us
in Sakrau stood a few barracks
it was a small labor camp
guarded by the German police
not yet by the SS
zwangsarbeitslager Sakrau
labor camp Sakrau

2

---

sei froh dass
du noch lebst

I remember that on a Sunday

2 or 3 days after our arrival in Sakrau
we were gathered on the *appellplatz*
the roll-call area
the camp commander spoke
'jetzt werden wir alle fröhlich sein'
'now we'll all be merry'
he laughed
'sind künstler unter euch? jemand der singen kann?'
'any artists among you? anyone who can sing?'
4 or 5 Dutchmen raised their hands
they sang and imitated instruments
they performed '*Tiger Rag*'
the camp commander walked with rigid steps
nodding into the faces of us prisoners
he stopped in front of a man whose head hung low
with his index finger he pushed into the man's forehead
'sei froh dass du nog lebst'
'be glad you're still alive'
        he knew what happened at Auschwitz
        he knew that in Koźle we'd escaped
        the first selection

the guards demanded that we write postcards

on one of the first Sundays in Sakrau
'to who?' we asked
'to who you want where you want and
write what you want'
and so we wrote
I don't know what
something like
'it's Sunday the weather is nice
father is well
mother is in a different camp
I hope you're well
see you soon'

I wrote about mother because I didn't know
about the gas chambers
thousands of postcards sent to all the places
prisoners came from
sent to appease the recipients
make those sentenced to death write letters
to assuage the next victims

I remember I sent a card to Maria
the woman who owned a grocery store
2 doors down from us
Maria was not Jewish
after the war I saw my postcard
when she received it she told our neighbors
'I got a postcard from Toshek
he's ok'

from Sakrau we were brought to Spytkowice

a new camp
there was nothing there
no barracks no beds no straw mattresses
we had to get water with buckets
no running water
lice
we got sick from typhus
every day dozens of people died
in the morning in the bunk beds
       nothing moved
       nobody moved there was no movement
       at all
       everyone was dead

the work was hard
we built a bridge over a highway
after 6 weeks only a handful of prisoners survived
due to the labor
the lice
the disease
and the beatings

in Spytkowice I got an abscess on my throat
it grew large
a prisoner who was a doctor advised me to
fill a sock with warm sand and knot it
around my neck to ripen the infection
so I did

one day a guard asked me what I had around my neck
he told me to take the sock off
the boil was very swollen and almost 'ripe'
he pulled out his knife and
in one swipe pierced it open
pus sprayed out
I was terrified
even though he'd barely given me the time
to be afraid
that's how fast he'd stabbed
at my neck

42

the entire time we were imprisoned we'd kept our own clothes on

a Star of David was cut out of the fronts and backs of our jackets
under the missing fabric a yellow cloth was sown
how could you escape with such a jacket on?
even if you removed the yellow fabric
gaping holes remained
in the shape of a Star of David
outing you to the world

for a year and a half we were transported from one camp to another

Trzebinia was next
20 kilometers from Auschwitz and
5 kilometers from Chrzanów

my father was born in Chrzanów
born in a family of ironworkers
dubbed 'the iron Schiffs'

when we arrived in Trzebinia the Jewish people in the area still had
somewhat of a normal life like we did in Antwerp before deportations
they wore a black band with a yellow Star of David on their arms
I saw it one day when they took us to Chrzanów
to delice our bodies and wash our clothes
which also brimmed with lice
the Jewish townspeople stood on the sidewalk
they gave us pieces of bread
father pointed out where his uncle's iron shop was
it was a Friday
what went through their heads when they saw us?
I don't know

if someone died in the Trzebinia camp
he was buried in the Jewish cemetery of Chrzanów
the dead body was placed on a carriage
and the *chevra kadisha*
those who tend to the deceased
brought him to the town
my friend Nathan Ramet's father died there
on Tuesday December 29 1942[3]
he was 56 years old
he lies buried in Chrzanów

a few weeks later
over the course of 2 days
the nazis murdered approximately
30,000 Jewish people
in my birthplace of Tarnów

among the dead
       my mother's entire family
       a family of over 100 people
       everyone was killed

father hailed from a family of 8 children
mother too
one of my father's brothers had left for Palestine in 1923
and 2 of his sisters emigrated to Belgium
except for them no one else survived
it lasted 2 days
they executed people
       in the streets of Tarnów
       in their homes
many were deported
the bloodbath of Tarnów

after the war I met Simcha Schönberg in Antwerp
he told me that in September of 1939
the SS captured 30 teenagers in the town of Brzesko
among them my father's youngest brother
they brought them to a football field
pushed them into the goal
and shot them
Simcha Schönberg laid in that goal
surrounded by the bodies of friends and strangers
he was lucky to just have gotten injured
he lay very very still
as if he were dead
and ran away in the nighttime

not far from Spytkowice lies the town of Sosnowiec

prisoners sent to build train tracks could see
the girls from Sosnowiec take the train
to work in an ammunition factory
they wore the star
we envied their ability to move around
the raids in Chrzanów collided with those in Sosnowiec
both places were now considered *judenfrei*
free of Jews

father and me and the few survivors of Spytkowice

were transferred to Trzebinia in February of 1943
we were there until November 3
the camp was surrounded by barbed wire
I worked on the railroad

in groups of 10 or 12 men
we lifted 8-meter-long rails
the ground was frozen and piled with snow
we could barely stand up straight
our arms shook knees buckled fingers faltered
the guards whipped us with iron cords that
had been used to keep the rails together
our blood streamed into the snow
clouding the white to a
muddied pink

the snow stuck to our feet
we didn't have real shoes
instead we wore a wooden sole
with an upper piece attached to it
every step lifted up snow
it stuck to a part of the sole
like the keel of a boat
we had no balance
we slipped
          fell
it was impossible to stay upright

I remember
a train slowed down and stopped
an international train going from Berlin to Warsaw
a woman sat by the window
a little girl sat across from her
the woman peeled an orange
I watched
frozen
20 degrees below zero
watching this delightfully heated train compartment

the glass was clear it wasn't covered in frost
why am I here? I thought
why am I surrounded by machine guns?
why can't I go home?
why are we here?

I dropped a *schwelle*
a wooden railway sleeper
on my leg
hurt myself intentionally
I wanted to die
my leg bled and swelled
they brought me to the *revier*
the barrack for sick prisoners
without anesthesia they cut away the mangled flesh
I was in bad shape
I didn't move from my wooden bunk in the barrack
I wanted it to stop
father stood in line for my rations

here I must tell you about Nathan Ramet
he was 18 like me
he also brought me food
this means that after those long days of hard labor
he stood in line a second time and
waited in the cold for my ration
he gave me that food
how can I ever forgive him?[4]

my fever continued to rise

one morning father brought me to the *revier*
there were about 20 sick people there
they took my temperature
it was 38.5°C
they said I had to work
like everyone else

I don't remember how I made it through
that workday in the frost
father supported me
he feared I would die
by the evening my temperature had risen
because of that father dragged me back to the *revier*
my fever was at 40°C
I could stay

I remember the moment a doctor came to see me
a French doctor his name was Waghchal
he was later shot while trying to escape
he gave me bread
the portions of those who had died
       in the bed below me
       in the bed above me
       in the bed next to me
each time the doctor said
'here another piece of bread because
this person died'

I was unconscious for 10 days
next to me laid Harry Spitz
an orchestra conductor
his wife was a singer named *'die Deutsche nachtigall'*
'the German nightingale'
her name was Erna Sack
she lived with their son in America
he had a photo of his son
'ich werde ihn nie wiedersehen'
'I'll never see him again'

he was a musician
after the war he lived in Hamburg
where he directed the municipal radio orchestra

I had to clean the *revier* windows
but the bowl of water kept falling
out of my hands
I didn't have the energy to lift it
then something happened
something unexpected
was it during Easter?
I don't remember
it was on a Sunday
there were many artists in the camp in Trzebinia
the German camp commander organized
a performance in the infirmary
it was the *'zum weissen rössl'* operetta
'the tavern of the white horse'

I sat in the first row and listened
to the singers who wore beautiful costumes
some dressed like women
some as men
they sang
to hear them sing in the camp was strange
their songs didn't fit there
sounded too beautiful
too alive
to mingle with cold and death
my mind wandered
dreamt even
'something else still exists' I thought
'something more
it might be worth it to survive
there is more than what surrounds me now'
experiencing that operetta in that environment
brought me back to life
by that time the deportation
had been lasting 8 months

my birthday

on April 25
I got a double portion of soup
got discharged from the *revier*
and had to go back to work

father looked at me
a skeleton hobbling out of the *revier*
that's when he decided to use the $70
hidden in our shoes
the money I'd been able to save
from the Gestapo in Bourges

for that money every day for a month
we got 1 bread and some sugar
I regained strength

in the camp there was a youth barrack
for people under 20 years old
when we returned in the evenings
exhausted and empty
I played melodies others requested on my harmonica
they sang along
it gave them a bit of courage
and warmed me

my ankle injury didn't heal
the wound remained infected
pus ran out
and now I should tell you
about this wound and about the flies

they said flies carried typhus

and that for 20 flies we'd get 1 extra
cup of soup
it was June
I placed myself in the sun
flies swarmed toward my wound
I didn't have to put in any effort
to catch them
I killed 100 or 150 flies
just by having my leg out

orders fly
flies fly
what a wonderful feeling
a beautiful sight
the SS is afraid
        afraid of typhus
        afraid of flies
        afraid of death
typhus death
the only one they fear

'flies carry typhus' they say
when Jews get typhus
2 birds
1 stone
but the SS can get it too

stupid concentration camp flies
concentration camp flies have no respect
no respect because
        SS or
        prisoners
they don't see the difference

orders fly
flies fly
the hunt is open

the hunt on flies
hunt on typhus
hunt on Jews
hunt on
                    SS?
the reward for flies is soup
20 flies equal
1 portion of soup

I catch flies easy
I'm envied
concentration camp envy
starvation-induced envy
because I have a gold mine
an inexhaustible oozing yellow gold mine
I'm wounded
for months my ankle has been injured
I've been hurting limping dragging and now
I'm envied

the bandage that covers my left foot
guards a true treasure
the wound infects
my ankle festers
day and night pus leaks from it
flies swarm
they stand in line
            in line for drippings of gold
            they can't get enough of it
they fly and fight for the finest piece
for any piece
in search of an undisturbed feast

their feasting feeds me
good flies

orders fly
20 flies for 1 extra portion of soup

flies don't know the difference
they don't show respect
SS   prisoners
all the same to them
the SS for once
is scared to death

I search for flies
they look for me
find me and I'm envied
because I don't catch flies
        I pluck them
they stand in line
swarm fly stand
in line
they nestle in delicious pus
good flies
20 flies equals 1 portion of soup

20 flies
40 flies
60 80 100 flies
soup for father soup for me soup for friends
I am envied

this party lasts for 14 days
        party for the flies
        party for me
and then it's over

orders fly
        fear passes
typhus gone
        flies free

                flies gone
        friends gone

I still have the festering wound
still have all the pus

in Trzebinia the grass stood high

on a Friday of that summer in 1943
I was working the railroad when I
saw someone throw a package
out of a train window
it was a newspaper rolled up into a ball
wrapped inside was the head of a chicken
the feathers and neck still attached

according to Jewish custom on Friday chicken is eaten
so that evening when we were back in the barracks
and everyone slept my father made
as best as was possible under the circumstances
chicken head soup
when it was ready he woke me up
together we ate the shabbat soup

the increased train traffic had outgrown the station

it had to be expanded
we had to dig new supply channels
for water for the locomotives
we dug the ditches in which
the pipes would be laid
a German company contracted the German
army to expand the station
who were the workers?
we were
the company paid the German army maybe
2 marks per day for each prisoner
the same way the SS paid the German railroads
for every prisoner transport
with discounted rates for groups

it was cold
our insides iced
minus 20°C minus 30°C
when the ground was too frozen for us to dig
the company's leadership wanted us to stay in the camp
so they didn't have to pay for our labor
the SS guards brought us to the construction site anyway
they demanded payment
we stood outside in the cold
whether we worked or not
the guards didn't care
they wanted to get paid
there were arguments
long arguments inside heated barracks
and we
we stood there
waiting
freezing
starving

our ears
our fingers
our toes

hardened and froze
some froze to death

I don't know who had the last word
the guards or the company
but it wasn't until hours later that
we were brought back to the prisoner barracks
where it was nearly as cold as outside

a while back in the Spytkowice camp

— I believe it was October or November of 1942
and it was already cold —
we'd kept our jackets on while working
we filled tilt carts with dirt
we were rushed
we had to keep a certain cadence
the guards ordered us to take off our coats
some did
some did not

at the end of the day when we returned
the camp commander
a member of the German *polizei*
stood at the camp entrance
the guard told him
'*sie waren faulpelze*
sie haben fast den ganzen tag ihren mantel
angelassen und nicht gearbeitet'
'they were lazy
they kept their coats on all day
and didn't work'
the commander ordered our group
to go to the *appellplatz* and sent for all other
prisoners to come out of the barracks
they had to stand around us

I stood in the first row like always
I wanted to see what would happen
I was curious
I was young
I always tried to have the opportunity to react
to respond to what was about to come

we stood in rows
the commander paced up and down in front of our group
spittle lined his lips and the corners of his mouth
in one hand he gripped a long leather whip

in the other the leash to which his German shepherd was attached
a rabid dog

'ihr dreckige schweine'
'dirty Jewish pigs
do you think the German state
feeds you so you can do nothing?
this is not a sanatorium!'
he walked back a few meters
'who did not take off their coat?'
I felt something deeply bad was about to happen
without thinking I stepped forward 2 steps
'herr kommandant
ich habe meinen mantel nicht ausgezogen
aber ich habe meine arbeit getan'
'I kept my coat on
but I completed my work'
he looked me straight in the eyes
'verschwinde in deine baracke!'
'get in your barrack!'

and then he flogged people
his dog bit the prisoners
it lasted minutes that felt like hours
all the men from our group were laid out on the floor
blood oozed from their heads and limbs
collecting on the floor
slowly merging together
they were all bloody
no exceptions
they couldn't escape the lashes
the guards and all the other prisoners watched
had to watch
while the commander continued to beat
the people on the ground

often
when a situation became critical
I took a chance and responded

however my body guided me
I tried to measure the pros and cons
'will he pull his gun?
probably not'
yes
any opportunity I saw
no matter how small
any premonition I had
of something terrible happening
pushed me to react
that rabid dog's head
when I saw it I knew
something was going to happen either way
so speaking up wasn't a real risk in that moment
If I hadn't said anything like the others
I'd have been beaten like the others
I wouldn't have escaped
by speaking up I placed myself in a different position
I tried to influence the outcome
I don't know if it was ever truly possible
but I tried

our lives didn't matter
they meant nothing

in the heart of the winter

the winter of 1943
during roll call
a Ukrainian guard noticed someone was missing
a young man from Antwerp
baker Wang's son from the Gulden Vliesstraat
he was sick and hid under his straw mattress
the guards found him
and brought him from the barracks

the entire camp was there
guards and prisoners
the Ukrainian guard brought him to the gate and
confiscated his cap and threw it in the air
there it flew
'hol deine mütze'
'go get your hat'
the boy took a few steps before
in one movement
the guard slung his gun from his shoulder
and shot a bullet
through the boy's head
that was the first time I saw someone
murder just like that

I also remember a man who was very small and skinny

I'm not that tall myself but this man
only reached my shoulders
mister Übersfeld
he wore large gloves which he had fashioned himself
I don't know how
it was cold
everything was frozen and our job
was to plow the ground with a shovel
mister Übersfeld was feeble
we all were
the shovel weighed more than him
he was sick and couldn't work
2 guards called him over
'you look like a doll with those gloves'
they hit him and threw him toward each other
they enjoyed themselves that way
until he was dead

'tod während der arbeit'
deceased while working
according to SS terminology
which meant that mister Übersfeld
hadn't fled

the numbers of prisoners
dead or alive
corresponded with the list of prisoners
that was the only thing that mattered
guards had their fun
we were like birds they could shoot at
with no repercussions
the hunt was on

I remember

it was summer and mister Pollack a textile producer
from Amsterdam who owned multiple homes
went around to the other prisoners
he took scraps of paper and wrote
'I'm selling you a house
located at this address in Amsterdam'
he added the prisoner's name and his signature
for 2 weeks this is how he was able to get
half a bread per day
in exchange for a house
under these conditions he sold many homes
and still
a few months later he was dead

after the war toward the end of the 50s
I met his son in Antwerp
I told him this story
no one ever came to claim any of the houses
his father traded for chunks of bread
the home buyers did not make it out of the camp alive

one cold morning I was trying to dig into the terrain

when a German armed with a weapon
stood next to me
'give me that spade'
he dug with great ease
I looked at him
lost my focus for a moment and said
'if I wasn't hungry and only had to dig once a day
I'd also be able to do that'
he dropped the spade
and beat me until I bled all over
I regretted speaking up

you know
I was 17 years old and rebelling
the guards thrashed people who were sick
they beat people who were wounded
whenever I reacted father said
'here everyone who wears an SS armband is a priori right
so keep your mouth shut
one time you will come across somebody
who won't tolerate your remarks
and you will not make it
keep your mouth shut'

the fact that I could express myself in German
helped me in many situations
the camp commander who looked me in the eye for 3 or 4 seconds
the one with his German shepherd in the story with the coats
was he a bit rattled because I spoke German?
it's possible
with 1 hand in the air he shouted
'verschwinde in deine baracke!'
it saved my life that time
we were pests to them
but sometimes the pests spoke their language
that confounded them for a second
and sometimes that was enough
to elicit a different behavior from them

those who didn't speak German had no opportunity
to defend themselves

the nazis had been taught to see us as less than nothing
we were vermin
not one guard had to answer for himself after killing us
he killed because he felt like killing in that moment
they had their doctrine
but because I spoke their language
in a flash their beliefs stumbled
a few times that moment of hesitation
was enough

I always addressed SS officers with
a higher ranking than they had
I tried to outsmart them
I combined everything I'd seen work to survive

2:00 am in Trzebinia

the guards shouted us awake
we were to give them all our leather possessions
shoes belts everything
the leather could be used in the war
for my 12th birthday
my mother gave me a *scoutskoppelriem*
a belt made up of 3 parts with 2 iron rings
I showed it to the guard and said
'*das ist eine kindergürtel*
lassen sie ihn mir'
'that's a children's belt
let me keep it'
it sounds unbelievable
but once again
the fact that I spoke German helped

I still have that belt
yes
I managed to take it from Birkenau
I fought for it and I have it
I don't remember what I did when I had to undress
in front of an SS doctor or SS officers
I don't remember how I was able to hide it
but I still have it
it connects me to my mother

'are you wearing your sister's shoe?'

one day I had to unload wagons heavy with gravel
I believe it was September 1943
a large German man stood next to me
tall and wide
his weight hung in lumps around his frame
he was a *meister* or other specialist representing the railroad company
'what do you have there?
are you wearing your sister's shoe?'
my foot was still swollen and couldn't fit in a clog
I wore a kind of slipper that I'd made myself
I showed him my foot and he said
'in diesem zustand kannst du nicht arbeiten
melde dich morgen früh bei mir'
'you can't work in this condition
come to me tomorrow morning'

the next day I went to the meeting place
the *meister* had asked the German guards if he
— under his responsibility — could take me
he brought me to a small wooden barrack
I was scared
I didn't know what he wanted from me
he told me to go inside
showed me his room
'you will clean the entire place and light the fire
so that I'm warm when I return from work
you will do this until you're healed'
he added
'du wirst doch nicht fliehen wollen?'
'you won't flee right?'

I did what he asked
I was able to read his newspaper
I read about the German army fighting near Stalingrad
read odes written by the people to the military
the same people who were guarding us
                              hurting us
                              killing us

I also fixed the door to his room
it dragged across the floor when first opened

in the evening the *meister* congratulated me on my work
he gave me a piece of bread and piece of meat
I cut the meat in 2 and put half in a piece of paper
'was machst du?
iss alles auf morgen bekommst du noch mehr'
'what are you doing?
eat both pieces tomorrow you'll get more'
'ich will meinen vater dieses stück bringen'
'that piece is for my father'

the *meister* was so overweight he wore a sort of girdle
the next day he asked me to help button it closed
I put my foot on his back
'pull!' he said
I pulled and managed to close it
he gave me food
'eat until you're full
I also brought food for your father'

it started to freeze outside and I thought
I wouldn't suffer
I really thought I'd make it through the war this way
the *meister* had told me so
I was full of hope
you have to understand I ate meat and soup every day
and so did my father who worked on the construction site
it was unexpected
the *meister* insisted I eat a lot and warned me to not get caught
with any food when I returned to the camp
he took me under his wing
he was friendly but he remained cautious
he didn't mention what was happening at the military front
neither did he mention how the situation was evolving
because if I ever got caught I'd be interrogated
and if I said anything it would be dangerous
for him too

it lasted a few weeks

until Wednesday November 3 1943
that day we were not woken up
at 4:00 am like we were used to
we were very surprised by this
only an hour later at 5:00 am did the clock ring
by 6:00 am we were at the *appellplatz*

about 300 of us prisoners
stood on the square
a small man in a brown coat approached
he carried a black briefcase
he wore a black hat
he stood before us
removed his hat and addressed us
in a polite and friendly manner
'meine herren!'
'gentlemen!'
our jaws sunk open

we were always shouted at
'dirty Jews!' 'swines!'
but this man
'meine herren
da der winter naht und viele menschen aufgrund der
schlechten arbeitsbedingungen im letzten winter leider
gestorben sind hat die deutsche regierung beschlossen
euch in eine fabrik zu schicken'
'since many people died last year
due to the bad working conditions
the German government has decided
to transfer you to a factory'

sometimes
without naming the camp
the Polish prisoners referred to Birkenau
which was 20 kilometers away
they pointed a finger and said
'there you walk in like this and leave like that'

as they said this they motioned with their arm
first vertically then horizontally
we didn't understand what they meant

the man in the hat continued
'da ist eine schuhfabrik in Birkenau
wo sie in gut geheizten werkstätten arbeiten
werden und genug zu essen bekommen'
'there is a shoe factory in Birkenau
where you'll work in well-heated workshops
and will receive enough food'
the word Birkenau slid out in passing
like a slip of the tongue

'meine herren es ist 6 uhr wir sehen uns hier um 7 wieder'
'gentlemen it's 6:00 am we'll see each other here again at 7:00 am'
he continued in his friendly tone
'you can leave all your things here
since you'll receive new clothes
see you later gentlemen
see you soon'

we couldn't believe it
finally we'd work in good conditions!
no more deaths!
we didn't understand a thing
everyone had questions
we hugged each other
and celebrated
and I thought of the fat *meister*
I was leaving behind
I ran to the kitchen and grabbed a turnip
and a pair of shoes I saw lying around

3

hunger

at 7:00 am we were gathered at the *appellplatz*

with the *lagerälteste** prisoner Herschel
who was the camp's prisoner commander
he used to be a director at the Salamander shoe factory in Germany
he was Jewish
the top-ranking prisoner in the camp
life and death depended on him
if he wasn't satisfied with our work
he punished us by assigning us even harder work
work in places where prisoners died like flies

the camp gate opened and a large military truck backed in
the tarp was lifted and about 20 SS officers
with skulls on their uniforms jumped out
they were armed with machine guns
and whips
they yelled
'everyone line up!'
and our Jewish commander shouted at us
'*rechstum!*'
he was immediately punched in the face
by an SS officer who yelled
'*du da rein in die reihe!*'
'get back in line!'
we were so confused
but because of the food the fat *meister* had given me
my brain was functioning normally again
and when I saw what happened
      they hit Herschel
      they hit a man who decided between life and death
I understood something wasn't right

---

*   Within the concentration camp system, the SS implemented a prisoner hierarchy. Prisoners (usually those arrested on criminal or political charges) were given roles to keep other prisoners in line. The highest position a prisoner could reach was *Lagerälteste*, who reported to the camp commander and was responsible for executing SS orders, however brutal. Prisoners in these types of roles had access to privileges, which could include food, clothing, or sleeping in a real bed. This led to a rivalry among prisoners over roles that could provide means to help one survive and was part of the SS's strategy to keep prisoners divided.—Trans.

I understood the speech made by the man in the brown coat
did not align with what was happening

guards brought out the sick prisoners
and told them to get in the truck
an SS officer said
'those who can no longer walk
or who are sick can get in'

led by the truck the parade started moving
I walked next to father
but still had a swollen foot
I limped until the truck stopped for the first time
and then got on
I sat in the back
close to the opening of the tarp
curious as always
positioned so I could see outside
the truck drove very slowly
we were surrounded by SS officers
when prisoners fell behind they were forced to keep up
this was the second selection
we were completely unaware

Birkenau

after an hour the truck stopped again
and an SS officer said
'diejenigen die nicht mehr laufen können steigen in der lastwagen'
'those who can't keep up have to get in the truck'
slowly
       little by little
              the truck picked up speed
              father's shape became smaller and smaller
                    until the entire group disappeared in the distance

after about half an hour
we drove alongside barbed wire that snaked for kilometers
a frightening sight
I'd never seen anything like it before
the truck stopped by an entrance
we'd arrived at Birkenau

was the driver required to write a report
or did he go to buy a pack of cigarettes
in the SS office?
I don't know
a young man in a striped outfit came to stand near me
he grabbed my wrist and said in French
'jump off right now'
'no my legs hurt'
I didn't want to leave the truck
he pulled at me
'I need to grab my shoes!' I yelled
'you don't need anything get off right now'
the truck's motor started up and
he grabbed me by the wrist
that boy pulled me off
I fell to the ground in the snow
he hadn't let me go
I laid there as he walked away
I never saw him again
he knew what was going to happen
he saved my life

konzentrationslager

I stayed near the main entrance
and waited for my father
group after group of prisoners enter the camp
that day the Germans liquidated
the *zwangsarbeitslager*
labor camps
to collect prisoners in the *konzentrationslager*
concentration camps

my father's group arrived 3 or 4 hours later
I slipped next to him unnoticed
we had to go into an enormous barrack
where about 2,000 of us were packed inside
standing on top of each other
to give you an idea of our situation
all you have to do is open up a can of sardines
that was what we looked like
people were pushed inside
there was no space

a moment later
a man dressed in black entered
he wore an armband with the word *kapo** printed on it
we didn't know what that meant
he stood on a small step
held a heavy stick in his hand
and insulted us
'sons of bitches who the hell do you think you are
there is no laughing here

---

*   *Kapos* were known for their brutality, viciousness, and lack of scruples. Prisoners were selected by the SS for the role because of those qualities. Many *kapos* felt trapped as they were prisoners themselves and also part of the systemic violence and oppression. Heinrich Himmler, *Reichsführer* of the SS, said, in a speech given in 1944 to Major Generals of the German Army (Wermacht), "The moment [a prisoner] becomes a *Kapo*, he no longer sleeps with [other prisoners]. He is held accountable for the performance of the work. . . . So, he must drive his men. The moment we become dissatisfied with him, he is no longer *Kapo*, he's back to sleeping with his men. And he knows that he will be beaten to death by them the first night" (http://www.camps.bbk.ac.uk/documents/065-the-ss-perspective.html).—Trans.

it's over
here you'll work
you'll suffer'
he cursed us out in Yiddish
I'd never heard such vicious words
but to keep his job
he had to show the SS
he could do it

we were cramped in the barrack
unable to move
the *kapo* shouted
'I'm going to count to 3 and on 3 you all have to sit'
I thought it impossible that we could sit where we stood
given that the body takes up more space when seated
but I learned that it is possible

after 1 minute the *kapo* stomped between us with his stick
he struck and hurt people
you can sit where you stand
once you've been beaten enough
everyone sat down
he yelled
'don't move
here you must obey and do as you're told
nobody move'

that's how that November 3rd went
we sat there
he walked in and out
it lasted the entire night
we sat there
exhausted
like cattle
we didn't receive anything to drink
or any food
I don't have the words to describe that night

the next morning the *kapo* opened the doors
we had to get out and march in rows of 10

I walked next to father
it was already cold

Birkenau was a strange and unfamiliar place
we turned a corner and then had to walk very fast
there stood an *SS doktor*
probably Mengele*
and SS officers
next to me walked a boy named Sicherman
whose father was a watchmaker in Antwerp
he wore a red scarf
he was young about my age
I walked almost normally in spite of my injured foot
the feeling in my gut told me to follow the order
to walk as best as I could
'take off your scarf' I said to Sicherman
'no I'm cold' he said
I'd said that because I noticed in front of us
they were splitting the rows
some of us had to go left
and others right

we marched in front of the *SS doktor*
I didn't know what was happening
but I bit through my injury and marched like the best soldier
with a flick of his hand Mengele
ordered us 1 by 1
            in a particular direction
                    left or right
the boy with the red scarf was directed away from our row
together with about half of our group
they stood on the other side next to the elders
and the sick from Trzebinia who had traveled in the truck
that's when I saw them again

---

*   Josef Mengele was an SS officer and physician. At Auschwitz, he was one of the doctors who selected victims to be killed in the gas chambers. He also performed inhumane experiments on prisoners, which resulted in death, disfigurement, or disability. If prisoners didn't die from the experimental procedures, they were often murdered to facilitate postmortem examination. Mengele is also known as the "Angel of Death."—Trans.

it was the third selection
the selection which
without knowing
   father and I escaped

number 160275

of that group of about 2,000 men
only a few hundred remained
we were brought away and made to stand in alphabetical order
they merged us with another group
2 men held onto our arm and a third tattooed
our new identity on our skin
with a needle dipped in blue acid
my number is 160275
father's is 160276
it hurt
we were branded
but compared to what awaited us
this was nothing

Aäron Rosler
my uncle
was the last prisoner whose name started with the letter R
his number was 160274
I was the first of the prisoners whose names started with an S
we were in camp D in Birkenau
the *quarantäne* camp
to the right of the entrance
further down were the gas chambers
and cremation ovens

while they tattooed me I asked
what would happen to those the *SS doktor*
had separated from our small group
the man who tattooed me said
'you see that smoke over there
within an hour they'll be smoke too'
I didn't understand
I didn't insist

they filled out files with our
name date of birth job function
and date of arrival at Birkenau

those files were partly destroyed by the SS
when prisoners were sent to the gas chambers
they made the numbers of those who were selected disappear
at least that's what I think
because I haven't been able to
find my father's file
but I found my sister's file
she was there
her name right there on the page
in the Auschwitz *sterbebücher*

father and I were in barrack 18
in Birkenau the barracks were enormous
I can't remember how many bunks there were
we slept in groups of 8
if 1 person moved or turned around
the others had to follow their movement
there were 3 rows of wooden beds
on top of each other
I can't give an exact number
but there were about 1,000 prisoners per barrack
in the middle between the bunks
a brick pipe ran the entire length
that pipe was 1 meter high and 1 meter wide
its purpose was to heat up the barrack but
was never turned on

on both sides between the pipe and the beds
ran a narrow hallway
that's where the *SS doktor* stood during a selection
not far from the barrack entrance
when it was time for him to select
who would die or stay alive
we all had to gather in that hallway naked and in
formation walk through it and stop in front of the *doktor* in a group of 3
the *doktor* pointed to those who had to go to the gas chambers
that was the selection

no one could escape
because whoever dared jump over the pipe to the other hallway

where those who were already inspected stood
came into the firing range of an SS officer
who had the entire length of the pipe
in the aim of his machine gun

we weren't allowed to leave camp D
we wanted to know what they had done to the women and children
but the answer was glossed over
we didn't quite understand
actually
we didn't understand a thing

selection

one evening about 2 weeks after our arrival
it was announced that Jews had to stay in their beds
'juden gehen morgen nicht zur arbeit'
'Jews won't go to work tomorrow'
that night the man next to me said
'if they announce we can't go outside tomorrow
that means there will be a selection
when it's your turn walk as straight as possible
with your head high
present yourself as strong as possible
that is all
or no
those who will be pointed at
will not be here tomorrow evening
there are gas chambers
everyone can see the chimneys and the smoke
coming from the cremation ovens
they gas the weakest ones
the women and children
and burn them'

you hear this man
you believe what he says
but your brain refuses to accept it
because I hadn't realized
that the first selection had taken place in Koźle
when the SS officer shouted
'männer raus! frauen und kinder bleiben!'
the entire time we were in the smaller camps
we were sure that the women and children were in other camps
we were convinced that was the case

but that night in Birkenau I understood
the women had been killed immediately
along with their children
there were no labor camps for them

and

let's wait a moment
before we continue

I'd like to say something about the hunger

how can a person describe hunger?
it's almost impossible

I remember one day in Sakrau
we pushed wheelbarrows thick with gravel
I said to myself
'to not lose hope today I'll think about my 12th birthday'
it was impossible
I couldn't even think about it for 1 minute
because immediately
hunger took over
           took control

in the evening bread was distributed to be eaten the next morning
I placed the piece under my coat and told myself
'I don't need this piece
I'll take a tiny bit before falling asleep'
those small pieces of bread
never saw the morning light
the head could not rest
without eating
that means that we went to work every morning
with just a few gulps of watery coffee in our stomachs

the ration system was meant to weaken us
and to prevent us from being able to organize or resist
there was resistance from
           those who unloaded the wagons
           (they found the storage rooms for food)
           those who worked in the gas chambers
           those who pulled out the teeth of the dead
           the *sonderkommandos*
but the largest mass of prisoners
was so starved that the idea of resisting
couldn't even sprout in our minds

the Germans knew that
they'd calculated it

there were guards but their amount compared to
the volume of captives meant nothing
people sometimes wonder how it was possible
that such a small group of SS officers
could guard such an enormous population of prisoners
the hunger disabled our brains
we were busy trying to survive
'selbsterhaltungstrieb'
'survival instinct'

instead of our brain
a piece of bread inhabited
our heads

the most absurd thing happened
I don't know how to express it
it was a Saturday
Christmas in 1943
the prisoners under 20 years old were summoned
they gave us a little packet with 1 cookie inside

in between selections
the cookie packets of Auschwitz
you wouldn't even imagine this in a script for a play
cookies in Auschwitz!
they looked like *petit beurres*
we pushed each other out of the way to get one

there were lots of Polish people in Birkenau
they were also in camp D
they were allowed to receive packages sent by their families
meat chicken bread
they opened them right in front of us
while we died of starvation
I remember a man who yelled something like
'potrzebuję krawietz'
'I need a tailor'
I offered myself and asked what needed to get done
'fix these long pants well enough
and you get a piece of bread'

I sewed the pants
when I brought them back
he looked at them and said
'you're just as good of a tailor
as I am camp commander'
but he still gave me a piece of bread

how can a person describe hunger?

that abusive feeling
that ugly repulsive critter
it sits in the stomach angry
slithers up
            to the throat
            to the mouth

it gnaws it rages
creeps at the soft with its claws
slowly
upward
when it can't find anything
it snakes up higher
and higher
its claws pointy and steel-like
they dig in
grip
tear at the insides
at the soft and empty
the pain unrelenting
tearing the stomach to shreds
searching for something to eat
and on its way
all the way up
it lurks and discovers something soft
pulls drags rips
at a warm gray mass
eats it   devours it
until everything hurts
until my mind is emptied and
my spirit is gone and less and less
            I know what I'm saying
a curtain blurs my vision

hunger tears
it grips
scratches at the gray sticky mass

glides to the stomach
        pushes down
        pulls down
grabbing hold of anything it can find and
I buckle from the pain

I dream of bread
it's all I can see
        a plump loaf
        soft with crumbly crust
        the color of sun-kissed sand in a warm faraway place
my brain is gone
a yearning for bread lingers in its stead

hunger screams rages scratches
it hurts
it finds nothing
there is nothing
that freshly baked bread
can only be looked at
        it can't be reached
        it can't be tasted
        it can't be pulled at
        it can't be torn apart

hunger does not care to coexist
it encompasses
all senses alert
all senses focused on bread
all senses overpowered by the empty in our core
we see hunger
        we feel hunger
                we are hunger

the gnawing
hour after hour minute after minute
day and night always
we were crazed because of hunger
pained from hunger
we died from hunger

we were hunger
we ate ourselves from the inside
and there was nothing left to see from the out
we wasted away and died

I've tried to describe hunger but
hunger has no story
a story needs a brain to tell it
our brains were no longer there
our eyes looked inward
into the empty

hunger
pulling at the remains of a brain
tearing it up
scarfing it down
and in the vacant space left behind sits bread
we died of hunger
        yet in the remains of our minds we ate and ate
                chewed and swallowed
                        warm crusted loaves of bread
until toward the end
and only when nearing the end
hunger passes

a shadow gently clouds the senses
overshadows hunger
takes away the pain

merciful shadow
if only for a moment
I thank you
let me admire the empty
the space once filled with brain
let me dream of bread some more
with its textured outer layer
and soft sweetened middle
dear shadow
stay with me for a bit

how can a person describe hunger?
I remember after a selection
a friend from Antwerp named Apter
lay in the same bunk as me
he cried
said to me
'they pointed at me
they wrote down my number
I'll die within a few hours!
it can't be
is it possible?'

we talked for a while
I tried to console him
'maybe it's for a transport?'
but we both knew the truth

that afternoon he and hundreds of others were murdered
he had said
'you are here and I'm talking to you
it's not possible that they'll come for me
to bring me to the gas chamber'

Warsaw

sometimes we were sent outside the camp
to work on railroad maintenance
when new prisoner convoys arrived we had to step back
the trains rode slow and sometimes we saw faces
through the seams of the wagon walls
we heard sighs
        cries of children
        moans
when the train passed we had to get back to work
the people in the wagons had no idea
they had arrived at the end of their journeys
                the end of their lives
that it would only last a few more hours

I remember that after the uprising
in the Warsaw ghetto in December 1943
a number of us were sent to clean up the ghetto
father was part of that group and I wasn't
I went to the office to ask if we could stay together
'schreibe sie meine nummer mit auf die liste'
'write my number on that list too'
'ich kann deine nummer nicht dazu schreiben
aber ich kann deine vaters streichen'
'I can't add your number to the list
but I can remove your father's'
he replaced father's number
with that of someone who was dead*

we were happy we weren't separated
my uncle Aäron Rosler was sent to Warsaw[5]
going to Warsaw was good
there were no gas chambers
still prisoners died there too
from typhus from hunger
from dysentery[6]
from beatings

---

*   This was done by a fellow prisoner who worked at the camp office.—Trans.

4

father

Tuesday January 18 1944

the evening before Tuesday January 18 1944
the loudspeakers announced again
'juden gehen morgen nicht zur arbeit'
it was the 7th or 8th selection for us
we waited in the barracks
around 10:00 pm we had to undress
we all stood there naked
freezing
the *SS doktor* came in accompanied by an SS officer
we had to pass them in rows of threes
the *doktor* looked at each prisoner
he asked father very calmly
'wie alt sind die?'
'how old are you?'
father was 46 years old
'was für einen beruf haben sie?'
'what is your profession?'
he used the polite version of 'you' in German
a polite murderer
he wore white gloves
I remember it vividly
he pointed at father with his finger
then it was my turn
I stood next to father
I looked at the *SS doktor*
I knew father had just been selected
how do I express this?
I looked at the *SS doktor* intently
looked at him with every ounce of me
              with what little strength remained inside me
it could've been dangerous

I looked at him
I don't know
begged him
I don't know how I looked at that *doktor*
but he looked me straight in the eyes
and did not point at me

160276

the SS officer wrote down father's number
on an index card

we were in barrack 19 or maybe 18
sometimes I hesitate
that day 600 prisoners had to be selected to be gassed
that number was predetermined

in the first blocks of barracks the *SS doktor* selected
the sick and the weak
that wasn't hard given that we had to stand
in front of him naked
but if he didn't have the amount he needed
in the later blocks he also chose men who still
looked somewhat healthier

I remember a man in our block
he still looked strong
why was he selected?
I have only 1 answer
they hadn't reached their number

the *doktor* and SS officer left
I lay back down
because we weren't allowed outside

around 4:00 pm the bell rang

we were still in the barracks and they already came
to pick up those who were selected
I don't remember much from this goodbye
maybe I've blocked out this moment
the brain does not accept
the final goodbye

we weren't allowed outside
we were convinced they'd be killed quickly
but after a long time

the bell rang again
and we could leave the barracks

someone said the selected were still
in camp D in barrack 6
I went to look
the entrance was guarded by an SS officer

I don't know what came over me
I observed him for a few seconds and said
'mein vater ist da drin! lassen sie mich bitte rein'
'my father is in there! please let me in'

why did he let me in?
because I spoke perfect German?
he'd received an order to not let anyone out
but I'm sure no one had told him not to let anyone in
who would want to go inside?
it was absurd to want to enter
my eyes begged him
       I'd addressed him directly
was he moved by my ask?
he had a machine gun
how can a person know?
I'll never know

I searched for my father
there were 600 selected
almost all naked
I found father and spoke to him
and went back outside to the *schreibstube*
the camp office

usually the *SS doktor*
was accompanied by a prisoner
who wrote down the numbers
and that list was placed in the *schreibstube*
I wanted to get father's number off the list
'my father has been selected
write the number of someone dead on the list'

the man in the *schreibstube* said
'I don't have the list
there's nothing I can do'

I went to *kapos*
I went to barrack chefs who I didn't know
'*mein vater ist unter den selektionierten*
geben sie mir etwas zu essen für ihn'
'my father has been selected
give me something for him to eat'
I got cigarettes
someone gave me soup
somebody else gave me a piece of bread
I went back to the barrack
then returned to my block to 'organize' a blanket[7]
I brought it all to father
I don't remember how I did it
but there were so many dead
who no longer needed theirs
I stayed with him until the evening
until I had to go back for the daily count

the next day I did the same
I found food and brought it to father
this lasted 4 days
from Tuesday January 18 to Friday the 21st
a rumor circulated that in Auschwitz 1
— we were in Auschwitz 2 Birkenau —
a selection had also taken place
and that those who were selected could go back to their blocks
it was also said that there were discussions taking place
between politicians and the SS

this was the very first time that prisoners had to wait
4 days after a selection
it was extremely unusual
they were scratched off lists
they didn't receive any food
or anything to drink
some went crazy

it was awful

the Jewish Polish author and theater director
Meilech Herschkowitz
opened the door and asked a guard to kill him
— SS officers knew him because
on some Sundays he recited poems —
the guard shot a bullet through his head
right there in front of the door

among those 600 people
indescribable scenes took place
it lasted 4 days and 3 nights
father was calm
he sat on a bed
I sat next to him and cried

there was a small Jewish man there
who walked back and forth in an almost good mood
I asked him why
he said 'nothing will happen to me
they choose me at every selection
and then they let me go'
'how is that possible?'
he was very short extremely skinny
a skeleton a real *muzelman*[8]

if there was someone among those 600
who 'deserved' to be there it was him
skin on bone
he could barely walk upright
'I was sentenced to jail for 10 years
it's written in my file
I was convicted for stealing coal
they're going to get me out of here because I have to serve 10 years
I won't be gassed'
I didn't understand what he was saying

on the third afternoon
Friday January 21 1944

motorcyclists arrived
an SS officer entered barrack 6
and read 30 numbers
those 30
        among whom the small *muzelman* and
        an old man with a crutch whose mother was not Jewish
those 30 would not be gassed
they were allowed to leave the barrack

I sat down next to father
he stared at me calmly
he held my hand
I knew it was over
father said
'this is the fate of our people
I know I must die now
I'd be comforted and able to die in peace
if I knew you will survive this'

he repeated
'this is the fate of our people
we can't change it'

he hugged me tightly
he calmed me down

the SS came to get them
1 by 1 they walked out
then it was father's turn
I walked out next to him
the trucks arrived
the evening bell rang

he hugged me and said
'think of the story of Joseph and Potiphar'

those last words
'Joseph and Potiphar'
Joseph was in prison in Egypt and Potiphar was the warden
Potiphar's wife tried to seduce Joseph

but when she grabbed him he tore his clothes off and ran
those last words father spoke
'remember Joseph'
while he stood at that gate

I'll never understand
right before he'd said
'this is the fate of our people'

Joseph who pulls himself loose
that's the right way to live
to be in charge of your circumstances
able to make your own decisions
father could've said a million other things
but he said 'remember Joseph'
after spending days waiting for his death

the truck stood in front of the gate
the gas chamber was a bit further
he knew everything
and still

what could he have meant?
make up your own mind
take your responsibility
that's how I interpret it
        absolutely
        absolutely

that sentence
at the edge of death
my mother didn't have the time to say anything
she was gone before we realized it
but now
after waiting for death for 3 days
the last time I heard his voice
his last words

they climbed into the truck with difficulty
they were naked in the cold

I have to say I was only half conscious
I knew what was going to happen
and still I couldn't believe my eyes
I didn't want to believe

I stood next to the SS
they didn't have to shoot anyone
no one resisted

there was no resistance
people were already dead
the evening bell rang

I returned to my barrack
and after about 30 minutes
when the last truck left
we could go outside again

everything looked normal
I walked
in the distance I saw the smoke
rising from the crematorium chimney

I walked alongside the barracks
toward the gate from where I saw them leave
the secretary from the *schreibstube*
walked through the gate
he was a French Jewish man I'd spoken to
a few times
I went over to him
it was 6:00 pm and dark already
I asked him
wanted him to confirm what I already knew
'father left in one of the trucks
what happened to him?'

he said
'go back to your barrack and say the *kaddish*'
the prayer for the deceased

5

to outsmart it

in the weeks that followed father's death

everything was empty
everyone we knew
one after the other after the other
           disappeared
                       beaten
                                 murdered

we were empty
we were hungry
we told ourselves
'tomorrow is my turn
or the day after'
every day was just an extension
we knew that

I was lonely
for a year and a half father and me
had been together all the time
from morning to evening
and from evening to morning
he told me a lot in those months
the places we found ourselves in
meant he no longer had to speak to me as if I was a child
he didn't complain
not when he was sick or when his limbs bulbed
and bruised from injury and infection
complaints made the suffering worse
they sped up death
father encouraged others
he tried to continue to hope
even when there was none left

he was always present in my head
I felt he watched over me
I thought of the things he used to say
and felt his absence
           felt different
it was a loneliness that drowned

and still
the search for a piece of bread
got the upper hand
even though next to me
there was a permanent empty space

because we were in camp D

a *durchgangslager*
a transit camp
they often picked groups of men to work
in other camps around Auschwitz
we formed a supply of labor that could be put to work
as they pleased for the many smaller concentration camps
around Auschwitz

in February the SS decided to send prisoners
to the coal mine in Jawischowitz
a place everyone feared
I was part of the first group of 320 prisoners
they brought us to the showers near the gas chambers
and we passed a large group of Italians
there was a little girl with black curls
she was 4 or 5 years old
she clutched a doll
she smiled
she spoke with her father
her mother carried a baby in her arms
they had no idea

we showered in a large hall
doctors came to point out who was least equipped for labor
so that exactly 300 prisoners remained
once the choices were made they gave us different striped clothing
we had to get into trucks
we were counted again
we stood in rows of 5
an SS officer counted
          there were 301 of us
the *oberscharführer* got the same number
someone with a higher rank counted us again
          again the number was 301
the convoy commander came near our rows
and took me out of the group

I remember that I'd hidden my belt between my clothes
and that I'd been the first one out of the shower
in the hope that they hadn't swapped out the uniforms
so that I could retrieve my *scoutskoppelriem*
the gift from my mother
was that why he picked me from the group?

a guard brought me back to camp D
I'd been removed from the file
I don't know which order this officer had received
we were right by the gas chambers
would they add me to another file?
I thought my life was over

but I misjudged their system
I hadn't been selected
I still belonged to the mass
the thousands of prisoners

we passed the place where I'd seen the group of Italians
they were dead
naked and dead
spread on the floor
when I tell this story
I see the little girl with her doll
always
while we showered they were gassed
it lasted an hour
they lay there
on the ground
behind the barrack in which they'd been gassed

back in camp D I thought
'father is watching over me'
what did that mean?
that I had to look out for myself like he'd told me to?
that the attention I paid myself had to match the attention he paid me?
I don't know

Auschwitz 3

on Wednesday March 1 1944
I was transferred to Buna-Monowitz
a concentration camp located 6 kilometers from Auschwitz
also known as Auschwitz 3
I believe there were about 10,000 prisoners in Monowitz
the camp was built for a company named IG Farben
to make synthetic rubber
from butadiene and natrium
that's where the camp name Buna-Monowitz[9] came from

whenever we left the camp
always in rows of 5
an orchestra made up of prisoners stood by the gate
they played military marches
we had to march to the beat
the SS counted us
we left as numbered commandos
who went to work in the factory

I was in block 36
it was dirty
we worked to restore the barracks
it rained
we worked in the mud

we were hungry
we couldn't dry ourselves off
I was in bad shape

the *kapos* of the labor unit
worked for the SS and lived in block 4
the *prominentenblock*[10]
on Saturday and Sunday evenings there was a concert in block 4
with Harry Spitz as the conductor
I'd met him in the *revier* in Trzebinia
Spitz knew everybody
the SS officers the *kapos*

and prisoner camp commander Paul Kozwana
a criminal with number 39 tattooed on his arm
which showed he was one of the first prisoners in Auschwitz
number 39 always wore an impeccable black suit

we stayed away from block 4
avoided it
we were afraid of it

you know
the expression *'nicht auffallen'*
means 'don't stand out'
I often did the opposite
because I love music so much
one night I walked to block 4
to listen to the Waltz
Gronoud's *Orpheus in the Underworld*
it rained hard
I was soaked
I lay on the ground in the mud
listened
almost felt 'happy'
a hand grabbed me by the neck
'was treibst du hier?'
'what are you doing here?'
I was pulled to my feet
it was number 39 the prisoner camp commander
I wasn't sure which law I had defied
'ich höre nur die musik an'
'I'm just listening to the music'
he punched me in my stomach my face my chest
and screamed
'hau ab!'
'get out of here!'

— later when I became a cook I often saw him in block 4
by that time I was no longer afraid of him
because I was under the protection of an SS officer
one day I said to number 39

'do you remember that evening of the performance
when someone lay in the rain listening to the music?
you grabbed him by the collar
what did he do wrong?'
'everyone was supposed to be in their barracks'
'I was that prisoner' I said to him
it gave me a small bit of satisfaction —

in Buna there were also Polish people who were free
and a group of English prisoners of war
we weren't allowed to speak with them
the SS factory commander
the *oberscharführer*
was a man named Rakers[11]
an enormous man
a man who smiled when he saw pain
with hands the size of plates

one night
— we were on our way back from our work assignment —
we saw three gallows on the *appellplatz*
the SS had found pliers by 3 prisoners and
every attempt to escape was punished by death

everyone had to be present at the hanging
the 3 men stood next to each other
big lights were aimed at the gallows
it was sinister
Rakers stood in front of the 3 men
when they tied the nooses around their necks
the first man yelled
'*kopf hoch kameraden wir sind die letzte!*'
'keep your heads up comrades we're the last ones!'
I forgot what the second man yelled
the third said
'*es lebe die freiheit!*'
'long live freedom!'

when the trap door was opened
        the moment the body fell

Rakers grabbed that man by his ankles
he lifted him to prolong his struggle with death
as if he wanted to make clear
'in my presence
no one pronounces the word freedom'

Rakers had a ritual

he rode his bike past every barrack
to make sure there wasn't any food smuggled in
        woe the person who'd get caught
if we ran into Rakers and forgot to take off our cap
he rocked us to the ground with one punch

one morning
in May of 1994
we — as usual — walked in rows of 5 toward the gate
there stood Rakers leaning against his bike
he called me over
'komm hier!'
he said something like
'you rascal
why is your collar open?'

rascal?
it wasn't like him to use a rather friendly word
'er war geschlossen als ich aus dem lager kam
aber ich ausdachte dass ich ihn hier öffnen darf'
'it was tied when I left the camp
but I thought I could loosen it here'
he waved his giant hands in the air
'wenn du noch einmal hier vorbeikommst mit einem offenen kragen
dann gebe ich dir eine runter dass du glaubst dass dich ein pferd geschlagen hat'
'if you ever come by here with an open collar again
I'll hit you so hard you'll think you've been beaten by a horse'
'verstanden?'
'understand?'
'yes'
'wiederhole'
'repeat'
I slowly repeated the sentence
the further along I got
the more I imagined him beating me
getting closer and closer
to being stomped to death
by Rakers the horse

instead he burst out laughing
he slapped his thigh
called an SS guard
'Hans! listen to what he's saying'
I had to repeat the sentence
I saw it was going well
the weather was nice
the sky was clear
he was in a good mood
I repeated the sentence
the *kapo* of my unit came to see what was going on
he tried to strike me with his stick but Rakers said
'he'll be right there
it's nothing'

a few days later
he stood at the gate with his bike again
I looked away but when I passed him he grabbed me
by the shoulder to pull me out of the row
I was so surprised I forgot to take off my hat
'warum nimmst du deine mütze nicht ab?'
'why don't you take off your hat?'
I did what he asked
'ah! ich sehe!
wann warst du zum letzen mal beim friseur?'
'I see!
when was the last time you went to the barber?'
when we let out hair grow it could mean we planned to escape
'heute ist samstag und ich lasse sie jeden sonntag schneiden'
'today is Saturday and I get it cut every Sunday'
'wenn ich dich noch einmal mit solchen haaren sehe dann'
'make sure I don't see you with hair like this again!
otherwise'
that 'otherwise' was the worst threat
anything could follow
beatings   being sent to the mine death
but he didn't touch me
he said
'hau ab!'
'get lost!'

you see he was enjoying himself
orchestrating his personal play
I'd surprised him by speaking perfect German

the following Thursday
all prisoners younger than 20 years old
were assigned to a new unit in an enormous warehouse
alongside a group of Jewish Hungarians between 12 and 14 years old
the SS had decided to train them to become welding specialists
because IG Farben paid double the amount for specialists
compared to the work of unqualified slaves

there were crates in the warehouse
filled with rusted screws and bolts
we had to separate the bolts from the screws
submerge them in oil
and clean them until they were usable again
the Hungarian boys burned long iron pipes
into pieces with a welding machine
I filed the edges of those pieces

'achtung!'
someone shouted the order one morning
we immediately stood at attention for a group of German officials
they were dressed in spotless uniforms with golden and colorful insignias
high-ranking officers from the land sea and air force
some wore a small sword like knights
a few steps in front of them walked Rakers
why did those officials come?
did Rakers want to show them the young prisoners
were treated well?
I don't know

Rakers stopped on the opposite side of a work table
it was 15 meters long and at least 3 meters wide
'wie geht es dir?'
'how are you?'
I was shocked that he addressed me
'sehr gut die arbeit ist nicht schwer'
'very good the work is not difficult'

then on impulse I pointed to the big clock in the hangar
'aber die zeit vergeht einfach nicht'
'but the time doesn't pass'
I knew he wouldn't say anything to me
Rakers laughed and said
'komm morgen früh in mein buro
dann wirst du lauf junge der SS'
'come to my office tomorrow morning
and you'll become errand boy for the SS'
he left with the officials

the SS had their own small building on factory grounds

they ate lunch there
I was to be at their service
it was a dream
because if there was food for them
            there was also a little bit for me
a bread crumb sufficed
there was a radio there and it was warm

I once wrote this down
'I had to outsmart death
it became a kind of game'
you have to be smarter than death
to avoid it is not the right term
to outsmart it is the opposite of
'this is our fate'
I tried to find a solution when there was danger
it means I didn't let fate get its way

that day 2 of the young Hungarians were arguing next to me
they bickered about a welding torch and
suddenly one of the boys burned my cheek with the torch
they put some salve and stuck a large piece of gauze
to the open wound
when we left the factory in the evening
Rakers said to me
'so kannst du zu uns nicht kommen'
'you can't come to us looking like that'
they couldn't use anyone with a disfigured face
such a disappointment!
this happened in April or May of 1944
I was still in block 36
a German came to stand next to me
'ich bin der kapo der SS-schneider'
'I'm the *kapo* of the SS tailors'
he wasn't wearing his *kapo* vest
just regular camp attire
'I could give you SS underwear once in a while
the Polish people in the factory would be happy

to give you something in return
you could make a deal with them'
I wondered what that meant
was it a trap?
it scared me
'no thank you I'm not interested'

he grabbed me 2 days later
this time wearing his *kapo* vest
'I understand your hesitation
I'm risking more than you if I get caught with that underwear
I had someone who did this before but that's not possible anymore
there are people here who conduct business
try to find out what you can do
my name is Rudi'
he came inside my block
and gave me a package with a beautiful undershirt
'what do you want for this?' I asked
'it doesn't matter whatever you get for it'
I knew Rakers was lurking
but my hunger overpowered my fear

Rudi

I knew a Polish man I could speak to and took a chance
'I can give you an SS undershirt
what can you give me in return?'
such a shirt was rare merchandise for a Polish man
'I can get you bread a small pack of butter and 6 eggs'
'deal'
I'd forgotten what an egg looked like
the next day he brought me what he'd promised
back in the camp I gave the food to Rudi
'wait here' he said
he entered his block and came back out
I remember this scene clearly
            everything I share is present tense for me
            it never fully becomes the past
he gave me the bread half of the butter and 3 eggs
to him this was an obvious act
he trusted me
I told him I didn't need all of it
half the bread was enough
'if you don't take it I'll find someone else
take half
you're the one who did the work'
he didn't have to ask me again
even though stealing was punishable by death
for an SS shirt can you imagine!
I tucked my body into a hiding place
the entire bread 3 eggs plus the butter
were gone in a few minutes

sometimes I received schnapps or cigarettes for a shirt
I gave it all to Rudi
and he gave me bread
Rudi was a German social democrat
a political prisoner
since 1933 he'd spent time in various prisons and camps
he was born in Gera in the state of Thuringia
I would've liked to see him again after the war
I wrote to the city of Gera

118

but they hadn't heard from him
they didn't know if he survived

one night
someone placed their hand on my mouth so I wouldn't yell
it was Rudi
he brought apple sauce meat and warm potatoes in a container
it was more than I dared to dream of
I just fantasized about dry bread
in block 4 they had everything
but for me
that was my first dinner in 2 years

we became friends
        he was amazing
        thoughtful and layered
        he was kind
        höfflich
        very warm
since I was no longer starved
my brain reclaimed the vacant space in my head
the space previously consumed with bread and only bread
I was able to talk about other things besides hunger
Rudi wanted to learn more about Judaism
sometimes we conversed in the evenings
he asked about Jewish teachings and
because I'd studied at Yeshiva Etz Haïm
the Talmud college in Heide-Kalmthout
I could respond

work in the factory was rough
the *kapo* I told you about
severely beat us with his club while we worked
my life was in danger
I had to get out of there

a few times a week Rakers biked to the camp
one evening in July I saw him come in
and give his bike to a prisoner to watch over it

I walked over to that prisoner
'did you already eat?'
'no but I have to wait here'
'I already ate I'll watch the bike'
I waited for Rakers
it was night when he returned
I took off my cap and stood at attention
decided to address him directly
'herr oberscharführer darf ich sie bitte etwas fragen?'
'may I please ask you something'
he didn't respond
but turned toward me a bit
this movement indicated I could continue
it was strictly forbidden to address a member of the SS
'you chose me to work for you in the SS-tube in the factory
but that day my face was badly burned and you could no longer hire me
I don't mean to bother you but I am now in a terrible labor unit
where I am beaten every day
would you maybe be able to do something about this?'

he stood and listened
I felt emboldened to continue
I had thought about what he'd do to me
            shoot me?
            no
            beat me how I'd seen him beat other prisoners?
            it was worth it
while I spoke to him I thought
            I'm complaining to an SS officer about the *kapo*
            but who gives the orders?
            he does!
            thrashing was the rule and he gave the orders
            I'd come to the executioner to protest the beatings
            me the SS officer and the *kapo*
            a triangle of dark humor

Rakers said nothing
            did nothing
            took his bike and left
            he'd listened

a week later I had another labor assignment but
it didn't have anything to do with him
they placed me in commando 3
made up of about 700 prisoners
it was the most populous unit
the *kabelkommando*
we had to pull electric cables and I was the
'*laufjunge der kabelkommandos*'
errand boy

I had an iron ring with 150 numbered tags attached
each number had to be attached to a cable
it was a fantastic job because I got to move across the factory grounds
I was free to roam and sometimes even took the little train
that rode through the factory
but the most important thing was
I no longer had to fear the beatings
I now worked under the jurisdiction of the
commando 3 *kapo*

in the Buna factory there were English prisoners

we weren't allowed to speak to them
one morning I lingered at 6:00 am
on a ladder stood an Englishman
he heard me walk by and turned around
said very low
'we landed'
I didn't know English at the time
but the word 'land' sounds like the German *'landen'*
I understood

the English prisoners had succeeded in building a radio
and they'd heard that message that morning
I have to tell you
that in that moment I thought the war was over
imagine the hope
the hope![12]
I talked about it with Rudi
we were convinced that everything would move fast
and that the end was extremely near

6

train of death

herr rapportführer

later
on Friday the 5th or Saturday the 6th of September in 1944
I was on my way back from work at the factory
there stood Rakers — who'd become *rapportführer*
second-highest ranking in the camp —
next to the entrance
the camp lay lower than the factory
we were walking back and I'd seen his oppressive silhouette from far away
he wore his white gloves
I knew he was looking for me among the masses
I felt it

when he saw me he signaled that I should leave the line
he came down from the step on which he stood
I stopped in front of him
'*von morgen an arbeitest du in der küche*'
'starting tomorrow you work in the kitchen'
I said '*herr rapportführer seit ich mit ihnen gesprochen habe*
habe ich eine andere arbeit mir geht es besser'
'since I spoke with you I've gotten another job
things are better'
he looked at me and said
'*der winter naht ab heute wirst du in der küche arbeiten*
heute nacht wird jemand kommen und dich wecken
in welchen block bist du?'
'winter is coming as of today you work in the kitchen
tonight someone will wake you up
which block are you in?'
'in block 36
and my number is 160275'
'*um 3 uhr bist du in der küche*'
'at 3:00 am you'll be in the kitchen'

he insisted
'*der winter kommt*'
'winter is coming'
you know
these words from his mouth were like a mirage

that night at 3:00 am in block 36 a man shook me awake
everyone was asleep
it was completely dark
he brought me to the kitchen and asked me to help
carry a heavy tub of potatoes
the potatoes were to go in a peeling machine
I didn't have the strength to lift the tub
it weighed more than me
I dropped the potatoes
a piece of fingernail ripped off and bled
a doctor was called to bandage the wound
'gehe schlafen' he said
'go to sleep'

the next morning
the chef in the meat department took me under his wing
'we don't know what's going to happen
the war won't last forever but for now come with me'
in the refrigerator compartment hung an enormous amount of meat
I hadn't seen meat in such a long time
he cut off a portion and said
'go to the kitchen and throw this piece in one of your pots
when it comes back up you can eat it
only eat what I give you'
the piece weighed more than 1 kilo
I hadn't had that much meat in the entire 2 years in the camps

as chef I was allowed to move to block 4
I saw real beds one next to the other
white sheets
blankets
every bed had a lamp
next to every bed stood a drawer
it looked like a royal palace
'hier ist dein bett'
'here is your bed'
I was allowed to take a shower
a fantastic shower
everything that went through my mind when I lay in bed after
it was too much

one day number 39 the *lagerälteste*
thundered into the kitchen
he came at me
rolled up my sleeve and read my tattoo
'160275 was macht der in der küche!'
'what's he doing in the kitchen!'
he yelled
the kitchen *kapo* said
'Rakers hat ihn uns gebracht'
'Rakers brought him to us'
suddenly raging number 39 went quiet
I remember how he departed without another word
he knew he shouldn't question a decision made by Rakers

I prepared soup in 3 pots of 300 liters each
the portions were strictly regulated
but I could choose the seasoning
I can still see the large jars filled with spices
we had to wash the empty cooking pots with big metal brushes
the kitchens had to be impeccably clean by the evening
prisoners were barely fed but everything had to be spotless and
back in its exact place
                    it was an obsession

I remember once in a while we placed a pot of soup in front of block 4
and gave it to the other prisoners
in return they polished our shoes
and they got real soup

I forgot to say that my first day as a cook
I was brought to a warehouse filled with clothes
I got 3 white uniforms
undershirts shirts socks and white aprons
leather shoes that fit
handkerchiefs
I was transformed

and little by little

I became myself again
I regained my weight
my brain started to function again
clarity and the ability to reason returned
I recognized injustices again
there was a *kapo* who beat people for no reason
I went up to him
'why are you hitting this man?'
'what do you have to say about it?' he said
I pushed him into a water storage
a large tub that was there in case of fire
the *kapo* was afraid to respond
he feared my white uniform
            my stronger build
when I was around prisoners were beaten less
because people knew Rakers had chosen me

luck

what luck I had
such luck!
even though I helped it a little
we were about 20 cooks for thousands of prisoners
I couldn't have wished for a better situation
the cooks were almost all German prisoners
but I think there was also a French man
he'd been head chef on the *Normandie* ship
the other chefs had been prisoners for a long time
none of them had a tattoo that had more than 4 numbers
I ate refined foods meant for the SS camp commander

one day I was cleaning a pot while others unloaded the truck
a young SS officer stood behind me and struck me with his club
they usually didn't beat us in the kitchen
but I understood he wanted me to help unload
so I did
afterward I stood next to him without fear
he was the lowest-ranking member of the SS hierarchy
he'd hit me without reason
because I'd been working
he said 'come'
we went down to the basement
just us two
he spoke French
was he from the Alsace region?
'I'm going to ask you a question and you'll answer me
honestly and without fear'
'yes'
'when I hit you I knew that wasn't necessary
tell me what you would have done if you'd been able to respond?'
that was as close to an apology as he could get

I said
'you hit me and I stood back up
if I'd have hit you
you wouldn't have gotten up again'

when he posed his question I saw clearly
that I was allowed to respond
it was strange
he wanted to know what I thought of him

one day
I believe it was in September or October of 1944
yes
because I'd been working in the kitchen for a while
nazi camp leadership decided to celebrate
the third birthday of the Buna-Monowitz camp
a large tent was built in a corner of the camp
with benches for about 2,000 people
the prisoners worked for 2 days to dig a hole where the orchestra would play
a stage was built
everything was ready for the party in honor of Buna
the 'invitees' had to be properly dressed
we were the privileged ones in the camp
I can't remember what the orchestra played during the celebration
Beno Klein from Brussels impersonated Charlie Chaplin
the *Charlot* films were prohibited in nazi Germany
but his impression was so well done that the Germans shed tears from laughter
there were acrobats
a scene from a musical was re-enacted
many artists were imprisoned in the camp
suddenly someone called
'Toshek where are you?
your cousin Schloïme is here!'

> in a dirty barrack
> sick
> like a skeleton
> sat Schloïme
> he'd worked in the Jawischowitz coal mines
> they'd operated on his kidneys
> used him as a guinea pig
> his wound oozed from infection

I brought him food and went to the *schreibstube*
to request a new labor assignment for him

I went to Schloïme's *kapo* and gave him food
so he'd approve the assignment change

Schloïme was transferred to the *maler-kommando*
the painters commando
he had to paint *'rauchen verboten'*
'no smoking'
in large letters
the *kapo* treated him with deference
because I gave Schloïme food to give to him
after 3 months Schloïme hadn't finished painting the first 2 letters
but he regained strength
that was the difference between life and death

I could influence the behavior of certain *kapos*
by giving them extra rations of bread
we were privileged
eventually I no longer needed to work with Rudi
I gave him all the food he wanted
the roles were reversed
I ran a great but calculated risk
giving food to a *kapo* or prisoner was a grave infraction
it was theft and I could be sentenced to punishment
even to death

at the camp celebration

what I call the highlight of the 'party'
happened when a man with red hair and glasses arrived
he was Jewish German
the director of the *schreibstube*
he stood on stage and started a long speech
he painted the history of the camp
starting with the construction of factories
he shared how originally the camp seemed insignificant
as there were only 300 or 400 prisoners
to build barracks for the new ones
he quoted precise figures
      spoke of the second-year expansion
      lauded the camp's leadership
      the nazi discipline
he said
'we're currently at over 6,000 prisoners
and hope everything will go well
so we can continue to grow the camp
and double its capacity soon'
that man seemed so proud to be the secretary of a camp
with potential to clamp down on 10,000 prisoners
everyone applauded
as if we'd forgotten
      where we were
            what was being done
                  and what was happening
I listened to that speech
his words tumbling from his mouth exactly how I shared them
I'd been eating better and the fog had lifted from my mind
I was able to see
that this man was completely insane

10 days and 10 nights

in the kitchen we were able to read newspapers
we knew a Russian offensive was launched

during the night of Wednesday January 17
we heard cannon shots and bombardments
on Thursday January 18 the prisoners didn't go to work
they stayed on the *appellplatz*
I was in the kitchen
no one really understood what was happening
hours went by
the SS officers were nervous
it was very unusual
around 6:00 pm the announcement was made
'dieses lager wird evakuiert'
'this camp is being evacuated'

it was night when we left Buna-Monowitz
people had nothing
I had a coat

and since Rudi was *kapo* of the tailor unit
he'd had a uniform custom made for me
it fit me and was of a good quality
my pajama shirt was lined with silk
the same silk that lined the coat of SS camp commander Schwartz
today this fact makes me laugh
Rudi had gotten me that warm striped uniform
to help brave the winter
I even had tissues

our surroundings were awful
and in the kitchen there was luxury
yes

the guards ran in every direction
to push us to the exit
they shouted
it was a mess

we started to walk
outside was frozen
people died from the cold
I'd taken a 5-kilogram bag of sugar from the kitchen
and walked between Schloïme and Rudi
they supported me
I slept while I walked since I'd worked the night before
even though I wasn't weak
on the contrary
I'd regained my weight back for some time
but my leather shoes caused me to struggle
they were good to walk from block 4 to the kitchen
but in the snow they were awful
the SS killed everyone who lingered
                                who left their rows
                                who fell
every 30 seconds they were shooting

you know
the SS escort was light
maybe only 200 men
more was not necessary
we marched for about 24 hours

we arrived at a large station in Gleiwitz around midnight
I remember the wagons
dreary and sharp
I also remember how the SS camp commander murdered
prisoners who tried to hide with shots from his revolver
this happened as we climbed into the trains
the image of commander Schwartz
lighting up the night with the flame from his gun
is burned into my memory

there were about 7,500 prisoners on the train
120 of us pushed into each wagon
cattle wagons meant for 8 horses
we couldn't move an inch
there was no roof
just metal walls that rose 2 meters high

every wagon with prisoners was followed by a heated wagon
        in every corner of those stood an SS officer with a machine gun
                keeping an eye on us through a small opening

no food no water

the cold was boundless
it snowed
we couldn't sit
stood upright pressed against each other
some prisoners went insane
they bit the throats of their neighbors
they were starved
some had to be thrown overboard
some tried to scoop up a bit of snow
by attaching a small box to a rope
but SS guards shot at them

after the second night
when dawn broke the sky's skin
the train stopped
we carried those who'd died
to the wagons in the back

after laying the dead on top of each other
the survivors had to go back
to the wagons in the front
I can't even say that it was a grotesque job
since those who were still alive
were also dead
I'm not speaking of myself
I was one of few exceptions since for a while
I'd been able to eat more

our time on the train lasted 10 days and 10 nights
10 days without food
there was nothing
day after day
the wagons in the back
swelled with corpses

the train of death

I was together with Rudi
my cousin Schloïme
and 2 friends
Rudi was an ordinary prisoner again
kapos no longer mattered in the train
there were no people with ranks
                            with privileges
there were the nazis and
there was us

the bag of sugar was distributed
and we swallowed some snow when the train stopped
our mouths wide open
aimed at the sky
we ate the sugar sparingly because
we didn't know how long the transport would last
the others in our wagon only had snow to eat

they fell
they died
like flies
the soup in the camp was little more than water
but it kept us alive
in the winter frost coated the barrack walls
but we were still a bit covered
there was nothing in the train
nothing
people died from the cold
        from hunger
people died from exhaustion
        from disease
people died from everything
they died from being surrounded by death
a convoy of ghosts
of people who barely weighed 35 kilograms
we were a coffin on wheels
next to you behind you in front of you
there was death

you spoke to someone
and the next moment
he was no longer there
you spoke with the dead
while clinging onto life
on the train of death

10 days and 10 nights it lasted
not because the train rode the entire time
but because it also stopped
       to let military convoys pass
       to evade bombings
       and to move the dead

one morning
the train stood still at a station in northern Germany
our wagon was below a pedestrian bridge
teenagers between 12 and 15 years old walked across
maybe they were going to school
they stopped to look at us
the wagons with the living were as hideous to see
as those brimming with the dead
the living were no better off
starved and frozen
cramped and suffering
the living were skeletons
this is how it was
we were impossible to look at

the children on the bridge locked their eyes on us
they laughed
pointed their fingers at us
called their friends to join
'schaut euch diese juden an'
'look at those Jews there'
they threw insults sharp as ice
crafted with language borrowed from the stürmer*

---

*   *Der Stürmer* was a weekly German newspaper published from 1923 to 1945. It was filled with nazi propaganda.—Trans.

it's an image I can't forget
anyone who'd see such a scene
would run away vomiting
sick with what was seen
but those young people laughed

how is it possible to raise young humans
who can bear the sight of that which haunts?
an image that for the rest of their lives
should keep them up at night
scratching at the inside of eyelids
trying to erase

how was it possible?
we
we'd gotten used to it
seeing one another
hollow bodies floating
flesh draping bone
carcasses of our former self
but for the children
it should've been too disturbing
to watch

I'm no judge
but I can tell you that
many stopped
smiling at each other
slinging words that gutted

we arrived in Dora

a concentration camp in northern Germany
the SS let us out
I remember the small number of survivors
that struck me
only about 1,000 of us had survived
maybe 1,100
it didn't matter to the SS
what mattered was that the exact number
of evacuated prisoners was there
dead or alive

we threw ourselves at water
the prisoners of Dora gave us
bottles of 3 or 4 liters
I drank maybe 10 liters
the others as well
water!
water!
life
we were completely dehydrated

7

Dora

royal bed

they led us to an enormous hall
the theater hall of the camp
1,100 prisoners crowded together
one against the other
there was no room elsewhere
other convoys of evacuated camps were arriving

straw littered the floor
we were ordered to sit on the ground
I thought it impossible to sleep in those conditions
on the stage platform stood a large table
the nazis placed bread on it
multiple loaves
we weren't allowed on the stage
can you imagine?
all those loaves in front of starving people
they cut it
while our insides screamed
and in a long row
1 after the other
we waited to get a piece

when I got to the stage
I told the guard cutting the bread
'I was a cook in Buna
I see you have nothing to cook here
if you'll allow it I'd like to clean everything once you're done distributing
I'll wipe away the crumbs so everything is clean'
'was willst du?'
'what do you want?' he said
'I want nothing
just let me sleep on the table'
'done'

when the bread was gone
I climbed on the stage
collected the crumbs
and later when the lights were out

I laid on the table to sleep
I rolled my jacket into a pillow
below the stage people screamed
they were sick
they were dying
they urinated and defecated in place
if someone stood up he stepped on his neighbor
and I lay there on that table
a royal bed
eating crumbs

arbeitsdienst

in Dora V1s and V2s rockets were made
it was a top-secret factory
we worked in labor stations hidden deep in the mountain range
the labor shops had been hollowed in the bluff
they were connected by corridors and tunnels
referred to as *stollen*

in Dora my number was 108724
Rudi was no longer there
he'd disappeared
we'd lost sight of each other when we left the train wagon
Rudi
where was he? I don't know
it made me sad
we'd grown close
I'd become accustomed to his presence
we talked about everything
and now he was gone

there was a guard in the camp
an *arbeitsdienst*
he wore an olive green suit
and boots
I'd never seen a uniform like that before
on his uniform he wore the bandit-warfare badge*
in Auschwitz and Buna there hadn't been an *arbeitsdienst*
he selected people to work in the factories
where the V1s and V2s were made
the weapons with which Hitler wanted to change the tide
the names 'V1' and 'V2' weren't even said out loud
we were to swallow the words in our throats
there was iron discipline
if anything didn't function as planned

---

* The bandit-warfare badge was a decoration of nazi Germany awarded for participating in *Banden-bekämpfung* (bandit fighting). The term "bandit" referred to Jewish people, communists, and others who were considered enemies and posed a threat. The badge included a skull, crossed bones, sword, and swastika.—Trans.

the person held responsible was accused of sabotage
and murdered
it was hellish

one day 10 prisoners were sentenced to death
suspected of plotting sabotage
the SS knotted 10 ropes to a heavy iron bar
they looped the ropes around the prisoners' necks and
the bar was lifted by a crane
that's how they were hung
we all had to watch

by March our group was still in the theater hall
I was able to hide out in that room for a month
I didn't work during that time
it was a *pagaille* in the camp
the lack of organization worsened every day
because new prisoners kept coming in

one day the *arbeitsdienst* selected 300 prisoners
I was 1 of them
they brought us to the *appellplatz*
a large square
we knew we'd get sent to Ellerich
a place in the mountains
to dig new tunnels
in Ellerich injuries and deaths happened daily
almost no one returned from there

we stood on the *appellplatz*
close to the *kommandantur* barracks
and the SS started to write down the numbers
of those who had to go to Ellerich
I stood in the approximate middle of the group
next to a Czech friend
I said to myself
'if Rudi would walk by now
he'd be able to help me escape this work'
I didn't want to go to Ellerich
the SS chief kept getting closer

and I backed up
row after row
I put everything on everything
as long as my number wasn't written down
there was still hope to escape that transport
then I saw Rudi pass by
he walked at a calm steady pace
I called out to him
but not too loud
our eyes met from afar
we locked
it was everything to me
I couldn't move
I didn't have the right
his gaze was steel
he walked away

was he afraid? I don't know
that was the last time I saw him
I'd hoped he could do something
that was probably an illusion
in Buna he would've been able to help
but here he was no longer of value to them

I never saw him again
did he die in Dora?
dying was not difficult
he was an 'experienced' prisoner
but still
anything
everything
could happen

my Czech friend and me stepped back row by row
we were almost at the last row
behind us
I want to say between us and the SS office
there was an empty space of about 20 meters
I saw the SS chief coming closer

death encroaching
                        coming at me
I grabbed my friend's hand and we walked straight to the SS office
we marched so determined
they could've believed we'd received orders to walk there
we escaped the transport
I'd asked myself
            'what will they do if they catch me?
            send me to Ellerich
            but I'm already almost in Ellerich
            so they can't punish me worse than this'
my friend was afraid
still straight-backed we walked into the SS barrack
there were hallways and doors
we crossed them as if we knew the building
and walked out on the other side
plants lined the space between barracks
we dropped to the floor
and hid between them for the rest of the day

from where we sat I saw the SS commander march
I was afraid he'd catch us before the convoy left
thinking back I don't know how I dared to do such a thing
here we were
tucked into ourselves and muddied
surrounded by greens
I saw my Czech friend again in Prague in 1947

once an SS officer asked which one of us knew languages

'here is paper write down all the languages you know'
they needed translators because the convoys burst in from everywhere
camps from all corners of Europe were being evacuated
I wrote the languages I knew
French
Flemish
Belgian
Walloon
Dutch
Hollands
Luxembourgish
Yiddish
Hebrew
English
German
Polish
Russian
Aramaic
I had a list of 13 or 14 languages
for Belgium alone I had 5 or 6
where did I find the audacity?
in a flash I thought
            in front of me sits a 'god' who knows everything
            across from him a 'nobody' stands
            he who is and knows everything
            his knowledge lives in his gun
            he won't lower himself by asking a nobody a question like
            'what is Walloon?'
            thus admitting he doesn't know something
the SS guard didn't know the words Walloon or Hollands
I was chosen

you remember the speech celebrating 3 years of Monowitz
that madness
in Dora they really had to expand the camp
it was bursting at the seams
to start the barbed wire surrounding the camp had to be moved

the prisoners had to move the cinder blocks
in which the poles were erected
to get the poles out we had to dig around the blocks
and break them by hitting them with sledgehammers
the sledgehammers weighed as much as the people handling them
but they had to make it work

my job was to translate the orders from the SS
I did fine with Russian Polish and French people
thankfully I picked up languages quickly
and learned Polish in Auschwitz and Monowitz
the words I translated were not conversations
but short orders
it didn't last long
2 or 3 weeks
but it was a job that helped me survive

a French man came to me
he'd been an officer in his country's army
he had a 39°C fever
but the barrack for the sick was overflowing
and he couldn't stay
he was very sick and so skinny
he said
'Toby I can't work anymore'
I hid him for several days in an unfilled hole
in the mornings he came to me
and I hid him
the SS guarded us from far away
so it wasn't too risky

after a few days he was better
because he'd been able to rest
and I could bring him bread crumbs
he said
'I don't know if we'll survive this but
if you need anything after the war you can count on me'
he told me his family had a factory that made utensils
he wrote his name and address on a scrap of paper that I
lost a few days later

we stayed in Dora until April 1945

until the day they announced once again
the camp would be evacuated
later that day the trains came
Dora was history

the camp was overcrowded
there were thousands of prisoners
after experiencing the previous transport from Gleiwitz to Dora
I made sure I was the first to get in
and stood in a corner of the wagon
to avoid being pushed and crushed by other prisoners
the corner protected me
each prisoner received a can of food
the Germans were emptying their stock
I don't remember how we were able to open those cans
but when you're hungry
you find a way

high in the corner of the wagon a wooden plank was mounted
an old German soldier sat there
his legs dangled above my head
the weather was nice
the soldier sang
he trusted me with his bag filled with bread and cigarettes
'pass gut darauf'
'watch it closely'
he asked me to cut a piece of bread from the bag for him
and to pass him a cigarette
he was friendly
he foresaw the end of the war
and he had nothing to do with the SS

at night when everyone slept
I opened his bag and 'organized' a piece of bread
and at dawn a second piece that I ate fast
I did that every night
in the bag was a metal box sealed with tape
my fingers itched palms sticky

at night I removed the tape and carefully opened the box
cigarettes flowed out
a treasure
I 'borrowed' about 8 of them because
I didn't know where the transport was headed
or how long it would take
but mostly because I could trade 1 cigarette
for 2 portions of bread
the journey lasted 4 days

the train stopped I don't know where

everyone had to get out
and walk to Bergen-Belsen
the old soldier kept his eye on us from afar
at one point he said
'du hast deine arbeit gut gemacht'
'you did your job well'
and gave me 3 cigarettes
that was generous of him
I now had 11 cigarettes
8 'borrowed' plus 3 received

you know
I didn't know who he was
still don't
he might've been 60 years old

8

freedom

Bergen-Belsen

an endless base
that had served the tank soldiers
kilometers long
they brought us underground
to the 6th or 7th floor of a huge building
nothing functioned anymore
tens of thousands of new prisoners were brought from all over
there was barely any food
SS camp leadership probably hadn't expected
to be overrun like that

it was the end of days
we fought for food
when the meal cart arrived in the kitchen
it was stormed by prisoners
we were starved
the SS shot at us it was awful
one morning I found a paper cone
I thought it was filled with grits
I grabbed it and a bit further 'organized' water
I mixed everything
made a small fire
and when the grits were cooked I swallowed a spoonful
I spit it out right away
it was wood glue
cloying my mouth and throat shut

I felt the end was near
anything could happen
I had to pay attention
avoid conflicts
I was alone
I'd lost Rudi and later my cousin Schloïme when we left Dora
I went to the kitchen and told the *kapo*
'I'm a cook
I was a cook in Auschwitz

perhaps you have a job for me
whatever kind of work it is'
'yes we need someone
come here at midnight'

at midnight I went to the kitchen
from there the SS and *kapo* escorted our group of 20 prisoners out
we walked without seeing much
it was black out
after 30 minutes the *kapo* opened the door of a food pantry
we had to load food on a cart and
every prisoner had to carry a large bag of food on their back

I understood why they organized the food transport at night
during the day they were stormed by prisoners
we returned to the kitchen
walking in silence through the night
then a scene I still don't understand took place

I'll try to describe this night for you
it was April
no moon
the air dark as soil
suddenly
we heard a window creak open
and a scream in the darkness
a desperate scream
'Toshek! Toshek! where are you? where are you?'
it was Schloïme
everything stood still
the group stood still
'I'm here downstairs!' I yelled
he frenzied down the stairs
out of breath
he hugged me
asked
        'where have you been all those days?
        I was asleep and your father appeared in my dream

he asked me
'where is Toshek?
why did you leave him alone?'
'I don't know we were separated'
'open the window' your dad said
'he's down there'

exactly how I'm telling you now
completely impossible
there were 60,000 prisoners
and this is how we found each other again
I don't know how much longer I have to live
but I'll never understand that
his scream tore at the night
he was beside himself
everyone tried to calm him down
even the SS guards were perplexed
I don't believe in miracles
but how did he manage to find me
among the tens of thousands of prisoners?
I don't know
I'll never forget that moment
it was surreal

I don't know
I'm unable to render how impactful it was
I calmed him down
I was still on duty
'come to the kitchen tomorrow
I'll give you food
say you're coming for the cook from Auschwitz
go to sleep now
everything will be fine again
we'll stay together'

2 days later

on Friday the 13th or Saturday the 14th of April
there were less SS officers than usual
those who remained wore a white band around their arms

and

through the speakers they yelled
'dieses lager wird den alliierten übergeben'
'this camp will be handed over to the allies'
we didn't know what 'allies' meant
only a small group of guards remained
and we were 60,000 prisoners
we could've torn them to shreds
without them being able to do anything
but we were sick and wounded
prisoners died as they walked
corpses covered the camp grounds
we stepped over each other
over dead bodies
it was hard to tell who was still alive
those who were still breathing were half dead and starved
resistance sprouts in the brain
and we no longer had one

Sunday April 15th

I was at work in the kitchen
it was located on a higher floor with large windows so I had a good view
it was around 11:00 am when the camp commander entered
I was making soup in a large pot
he told the *kapo*
'*lass mich die suppe probieren*'
'let me try that soup'
I gave him a heavy ladle and someone handed him a tablespoon
he scooped soup from the ladle
lifted the spoon to his lips
        the door was thrown open

a guard hurried in and clapped his heels
'*herr kommandant!*
die Engländer sind da'
'the English are here'

my cousin spilled into the kitchen screaming
'we're free the English are here!'
he bounced in a frenzy
I grabbed him by the wrist and put my hand on his mouth
these were the last moments
we were in the unknown
the commander could still use his gun
I was afraid something would happen
'stay calm
hold on
these are the last seconds'
I held him with everything in me

and then

tanks crushed into the camp
burst through the gates
stomped on the barbed wire
they were followed by a line of jeeps
at the time I didn't know these vehicles were called jeeps

this I learned later
I didn't move
clamped my cousin's wrist
        tall military trucks rode in
        filled with English soldiers
they drove to the *appellplatz*
everything stood still

then

hundreds of prisoners
        a flurry of skin on bone
        a mass of almost-dead
ran toward one of the jeeps
and
with their hands lifted it
to the sky
barely alive prisoners
so close to their last sigh
together they lifted
the jeep gleamed above their heads

through the speakers
an English military officer's voice rang
'as of now you are free'
that message was translated to many languages

free

but

there were dead bodies scattered on the floor
our dead
they were everywhere
body after body after body after body
people who had died where they stood
died where they sat
unable to take another step
exhausted

beaten
starved
unable to move forward
or take one more breath

dead

the SS guards stood there

the commander and others
they handed their weapons to the English officer
the commander shouted to the prisoners
'aufheben!'
'pick up!'
the English officer didn't understand German but
he saw how the prisoners bent down to pick up the dead
he pointed to the SS guards
'you you you and you
take them!'

and then
the SS commander and guards bent down
they carried the bodies
we saw how those who acted like gods
bent their backs and picked up our dead
we watched those who acted like gods
carry our dead away

that's how it ended
that's how it was

the hunt

a few hours later
like a raging fever
the hunt for the *kapos* started
prisoners beat them
killed them
one *kapo* sought shelter in the kitchen
a boiling mob snatched him
armed with shovels and sticks
they hit him in his head
it happened in front of my eyes
the English allowed that for 1 day

and no one is shooting

the next night
the weather was nice
spring was in the air
we were allowed outside
I went to the fields next to the camp
and gave myself orders
'ok
I'm going to take 4 steps forward now
          because I want to
and once I'm there I'm going to turn around
and take 6 steps to the right'

but by the 4th step I stopped
to look around
          'nothing is happening
          no one is shooting'
I changed my order
'I'm now taking 8 steps to the left'
again I looked around after 3 or 4 steps
          'no one is shooting'

I changed the order again
'now I'm going backward a bit and then I'll go left again'
what an incredible feeling
'and now I'm going to walk around this field for a bit'
and no one gives orders
and no one says anything
and no one shoots

I can't describe it
can't put it into words
freedom
I thought
'I can go there
          and over there
I'm moving
walking where I want
and no one is shooting at me'

I lay down in the field
looked at the stars
now that I could lie there of my own account

in that field
on that grass

what lying down is
what that night was

in that field
on that grass

sadly
the feeling of liberation disappeared quickly
and in its place the empty settled
I was able to walk around but
I had no more family
I was alone

prisoners left the camp

they plundered cabinets in a neighboring town
thrust themselves at the food
and died from it

I continued to work in the kitchen at Bergen-Belsen
one day I asked the English if
I could deliver the meals to the SS guards
who were now prisoners themselves
2 men helped me carry a pot of 50 liters of good soup to their barrack
when I opened the door an SS officer yelled
'achtung!'
they all stood up for me
          including the commander
I placed the bowls on the table
filled up the soup ladle
and drizzled 3 drops in each bowl
the rest I poured back in the pot

Tobias Schiff's revenge

they said
'wir arbeiten hart und haben hunger'
'we work hard and are hungry'
I said
'I'm still giving you more
than you gave us
for years
we weren't allowed to address you
we couldn't say a thing and you
you led the camp
        where you beat us
        where you burnt us
everything was
fine for you
then'

'those were orders
if I didn't follow them

I'd be executed'
he lied
those who refused to work in the camps
risked being sent to the Russian front
but no member of the SS was forced
to dirty their hands with blood bone and ash

it was my small revenge

Antwerpen

a few days later we were grouped by nationality to organize our repatriation
a Belgian officer from Antwerp asked me a lot of questions
to find out whether I was really Belgian and from Antwerp
he asked me which monument stood on the Groenplaats
where the cathedral stood and so on
they took many precautions

the liberation of Bergen-Belsen
took place on Sunday April 15 1945
I left the camp on Wednesday April 25
my birthday
I turned 20

on Sunday April 29 I was in Belgium
we arrived in Mol
received 500 francs and 'identification papers'
a piece of cardboard with our names

we stepped into cabs the mayor of Antwerp
— Camille Huysmans —
had sent for us
they brought us to the Centraal Station
on the corner of the Quellinstraat and De Keyzerlei stood a man with a camera
he took the first photo
my cousin Schloïme and I went to the Lamorinierestraat
where the Jewish Tachkemoni school was
someone stopped me and said
'aren't you Toshek Schiff?'
'yes'
'you look just like your father'
a little further someone else approached me
'aren't you Pinkas Templer's grandson?'
'yes'
'how you look like your mother'
what I'm saying now is not all that important
but this is how it happened
someone told my cousin that his sister lived in Brussels
and gave him her address

at the station people gave us money
because we were still in our camp clothes
some people cried when they saw us

we took the train to Brussels
we didn't have to pay for a ticket
we got off in Brussel-Noord and took the tram
people stared at us
mouths open
the tram swerved through the streets
in one of the neighborhoods my cousin spotted his sister
'Paula!' he yelled
the conductor stopped the tram
they fell into each other
she pointed at me and asked Schloïme
'who's that?'
she didn't recognize me

9

small revenge

Paula told us Schloïme's wife and children lived hidden

in the Ardennes in a town named Godinne
and that my aunt Toni was also in that area
another of my father's sisters Aunt Mina
and her children Betty and Mina
were in a small village in that same region

the 3 of us took the train
Paula Schloïme and me
a grandly dressed lady sat across from us
she started crying when she saw us
she looked at us intently
and introduced herself as baroness
she said to Schloïme
'sir
I had a son who fought in the resistance
they murdered him
today he would've been the same age
as the young man beside you
are his parents still alive?'
'no'
she addressed me
'I have everything I need
I live in a castle
join me
you will be happy'
I remember that well
but didn't accept her invitation

in Godinne
we went to the house where Schloïme's wife and 2 sons lived
his wife was Swiss
Paula feared the shock would be too much
so she went in first
she told her sister-in-law
'Toshek has returned
he's here with me'
when I walked in she asked me
'do you have any news from Schloïme?'

'yes he's fine
he's out of the camp
we were together
we were freed together
and we are together
he's here with me
he's here too'
she crumpled

Schloïme's oldest son didn't recognize his father
'that's not my dad' Victor said
my cousin didn't look anything like
the photo his little one was used to seeing
Victor was 4 when his father was deported in 1943
his mom asked Schloïme to put on a coat
'see it's your dad'
'no this is not my dad'
when Schloïme put on a hat Victor said
'yes
that's my dad'

that afternoon Paula brought me to my aunt Toni
who lived hidden in Annevoie with her husband
and their daughter Estelle

aunt Toni fed me
when her child was put to bed
I shared what I'd experienced
I told them that no one
no one from our big family of about 100 people
would return
they'd all been murdered

we talked and cried all night long
and continued into the next day
aunt Toni thought she'd see her brothers again
her family   her tribe
they had no idea
the people of Annevoie didn't know

aunt Toni might've heard rumors
but she couldn't have imagined
losing her entire family
only her sister Mina
who had lived in hiding just like her
had survived
and one brother who left Poland in 1923
and lived in Palestine

I told them everything
the entire night
into the next day
nonstop
little Estelle slept[13]
when I was done my aunt said
'you're no longer alone
our home is your home
and Estelle is your little sister'
Estelle was 6 years old

I had a roof over my head

I had my little cousin I bonded with
it was May and the Ardennes are beautiful in the spring
I spoke to the people there
they looked at my shaved head with wonder
and asked many questions

I don't know if it's worth telling
a scene from those first days in Belgium
when I was in Namur at the Shavuot celebration
the remembrance of when Mozes received the Torah at Mount Sinai
the Jewish teenagers who'd been hidden in the area
organized a party at the citadel
from afar I saw people working
they were digging a ditch

I approached them and realized they were German prisoners
guarded by a few English soldiers
they worked with their shirts off
they chatted among themselves
they worked nonchalantly
I went up to an English soldier and said
'I was in the concentration camps for 3 years
let me at them'
'go'
I walked over to the prisoners
and thundered in German
like I'd heard them bark for years
they scrambled like roaches when
a switch is flicked and light floods
they pooled with sweat
heard their own language
the shouting screaming commanding
music I'd learned from them
orders they knew by heart
I was there
and I raged

another small revenge by Tobias Schiff

Shavuot

I joined the celebration
the presence of other people around my age
it warmed me
I felt it in my chest
it spread wide
I felt something close to hope
they sang in Hebrew
it sounded beautiful
their voices were full
I listened to them like
I'd listened to the operetta in the camp
do you remember?
that musical moment that made me think
'maybe life is worth living'

on the way back to my aunt
a jeep drove by
its hood was painted white with 2 red Stars of David
between the stars was the word *chaplain*
I didn't know what that meant
I waved at the jeep
it stopped
the driver was a Black soldier
and in the backseat sat a young military official
with a Star of David on his collar
'get in' he said
I asked him what *chaplain* meant
'rabbi
I'm going to the military base in Florennes
to celebrate Shavuot with the Jewish pilots
want to join?'
on the way I told him I'd just arrived a few days earlier
that I'd returned from the concentration camps

it was the beginning of May
the war wasn't completely over
I remember large topographic maps

lining the walls of the military tent
I'd never seen those before
they probably weren't meant for the public eye

after the service the young rabbi asked
if I wanted to talk about my deportation
he spoke to me in Yiddish
said
'you tell your story in Yiddish
and I'll translate to English'
and I spoke

when the party was over he accompanied me
to the jeep that was going to drive me to my aunt
the officials lived in small houses near the base
the driver stopped at every house
I received a lot of clothes
shirts underwear shoes sweaters everything
summer and winter clothing
at that time in Belgium nothing was available
the war wasn't over yet
and here
the jeep brimmed with
everything I needed

I tell this story because
that was the first time I became aware of
a feeling of solidarity
yes
that's it
the mind
how does one deal with that?
mother dead father dead
sister dead friends dead
I have to say it
if I'd been alone
without knowing that when I went to sleep
little Estelle was nearby

that my aunt and uncle were there
alive
it's possible that

it's hard to imagine
what I would have done

but knowing I had people put me at ease
I'm not sure how else to say it

distance

it was May 8
I was in Namur in front of the station
I remember this precisely
suddenly news spread that the war was over
people started singing and dancing
they fell in each other's arms
hugged the soldiers
I hung back under a gate
observed the scene
and
saw the distance that separated us

I couldn't participate in that collective joy
the war ending was fantastic
but the 'end' for me was at liberation
after 33 months
in the camps

it was as if I had a secret
     CONC
        ENTR
   ATION
      CAMP
of which I could barely speak
the distance between them and me was wide
I was far away
cradling other thoughts
other emotions
their feelings and mine had nothing in common
I observed
not critically but
I just watched
just like I'd watched cruel scenes
over and over
in the camps

I was happy for them
I knew what war and the ending of it meant
but to me the war wasn't over
and it will never be
I couldn't partake in their joy

my uncle was a diamond worker

the diamond trade started up again
before the war my father had taught me how to cleave
he'd always employed apprentices
I started work in June or July of 1945
it may have been August
I'm not sure
it was when we returned to Antwerp and got an apartment
I ran into mister Gottlob
the man who cried 'this is the end' when we were arrested
he was also a diamond worker
my uncle and he became associates
and I worked for them

life unfurled
step by step
I was still young
and regained energy

I don't know if I did it on purpose
but I suppressed a lot of my feelings
it wasn't a decision I'd made
it's just how it was
I buried myself in chess
as soon as I had a moment I played
oftentimes I created that moment
because you can't think of anything else but chess when you're playing
no other thought can interrupt your attention
the game demands all of you
100% or more
I clung to this
let it take hold of me
at the cost of me
and my family

I know it and I'll say it

I've neglected important things
chess prevented me from thinking

I didn't always have the urge to talk
but when asked a question about the camps
I answered
in a few seconds I knew
whether the question was a real one or not
       whether the person regretted asking that question
       or not

I told my children about my deportation
when they were too young
8 or 9 years old
they suffered because of this
too young to process it
now my children are adults
and still suffer from it

there are children of survivors who admonish their parents
for saying nothing or not enough
       or telling their stories too late
a bitter and constant reproach
but I talked about it too early
I think
I blame myself
I have no doubt I brought forth
       unbearable images

there is also a second issue that
threw their lives upside down
something I only recently realized
I speak of my children but also about
the children of survivors in general

they only know their grandparents from a book or movie
where do you go when your parents are mad?

to grandma
she hugs you
sits you on her lap
or to grandpa
who holds your hand and takes you for a walk
having grandparents is a part of life
for the fortunate among us there are 4 of them
4 corners of life that can
fill you up with sugared treats and love
ground you when life pulls at you so hard you no longer feel stable
teach you a lesson with a sharpness just soft enough to understand
but for the children of survivors
this doesn't exist
their grandparents were murdered

I never spoke about this with my children
I speak about it with other children when I testify in schools
grandparents fulfill an essential role in life
they have time to coddle
time to listen
a child can vent to grandmother
when the child comes home again
what the parents did is forgiven
          and forgotten

I've reproached myself often for talking
about the camps too early with my children
but I'm also sure
that my children still suffer from not having grandparents
no memories
no photos together

the nazis damaged our children
all of them
I used to hold myself fully responsible
regarding my little ones
but now realize
that the absence of grandparents
also contributed

my son told me

he regularly dreamed that
I stood in front of a firing squad
as guns were raised and sparks lit up the air
he threw himself in front of me
to save me from the bullets

my daughter once said

'I often thought
I should have been with you there together'

if my children had grandparents
they could've spoken about this with them
        dad talks about something that sparks fear
        grandma takes you in her arms
        she envelops you in her scent and warmth
        consoles you

in the dark

for over 40 years
I've never turned off the light at night
in front of my bed is a radio
all night long I listen to classical music
next to me is another radio
so I can listen to BBC news reports
between my hands sits a book
when I wake up
it's on my chest

if I turn off the light
I'm there again
in the camps
immediately
darkness is the camps
                it's the death of others
                and partly my own
in the dark
I can't sleep

this didn't happen to me right away
the older I become
                the closer I am to that part of my life

the time between liberation and today
seems so short

those years in Sakrau Spytkowice Trzebinia
keep coming closer
Birkenau Dora Bergen-Belsen
it's like I'm there again
right there
this is what it is
it's hard to explain[14]

whether I share my testimony or not
it consumes my mind
it's there

someone once asked

'have you ever tried
to remove that number on your arm?'

I said
'who can remove it
from my head?'[15]

a piece of me is always there

I feel it growing with time
even when I'm silent
it's there
I'm there

I visit schools to testify
I see young people listen
they absorb part of my story
they send hundreds of letters
reading them cracks something inside me
is it hope?
I think of the words of Elie Wiesel
'whoever listens to a witness
becomes a witness'

10

God

father was religious and me too

I walked where he walked
went to the Yeshiva
to study the Talmud

when I left the camps
I didn't ask myself
            'where was god?'

god or no god
I didn't wonder if god saved me
who am I that god should save me?

what about the others?
who were murdered
            in front of me
            next to me
            left
            right
            bludgeoned to death
            burnt hung executed
dead any and either way

who am I to say
'god saved me'
why would this statement be true?
me saved

while the good ones
            the better ones
            the children
                        were killed

I can believe in a god who might exist somewhere
and who once decided to create the universe
an expansion in which
our earth is just a crumb
and if our planet is so small

what does that make humankind?

we're so self-centered that we're convinced
a god exists who watches what each of us does
that's the type of god I can't believe in
a god who safeguards our existence
because if that god exists
s/he took a million and a half Jewish children
1 million 5 hundred thousand children
murdered
what does that mean?
today it's a statistic
1,500,000

do you remember the face of that little girl in Colombia?
little Omayra Sánchez Garzón* who got stuck in the mud
every TV station followed her fight against death
the earth latched on to her
for 3 days
she sunk deeper
until it was over
our hearts shook
we hoped
we followed the story
shared her fear
saw it deepen until
she sunk
we watched and cried
while they tried to save her
there was nothing left to do
the tools to save her weren't there
she was pulled inward
into the soil

it was horrendous

---

* Omayra Sánchez Garzón was a thirteen-year-old girl killed by the eruption of the Nevado del Ruiz volcano in Colombia in 1985, which killed nearly 23,000 people. A lahar demolished Omayra's home and pinned her beneath the debris. She was trapped in water for three days while relief workers tried to save her. They were unable to free her.—Trans.

in Auschwitz
there were plenty of tools
            plenty of murderers
to kill the children
a million and a half children
is that a statistic?
yes and
no no no no and no
that is that little girl
multiplied by a million and a half

1 and a half million children
that's 1 child plus another child plus another child plus another child plus
another child plus another child plus another child plus another child plus
another child plus another child plus another child plus another child plus
another child plus another child plus another child plus another child plus
another child plus another child plus another child plus another child plus
another child plus another child plus another child plus another child plus
another child plus another child plus another child plus another child plus
another child plus another child plus another child plus another child plus
another child plus another child plus another child plus another child plus
another child plus another child plus another child plus another child plus
another child plus another child plus another child plus another child plus
another child plus another child plus another child plus another child plus
another child plus another child plus another child plus another child plus
another child plus another child plus another child plus another child plus
another child plus another child plus another child plus another child plus
another child plus another child plus another child plus another child plus
another child plus another child plus another child plus another child plus
another child plus another child plus another child plus another child plus
another child plus another child plus another child plus another child plus
another child plus another child plus another child plus another child plus
another child plus another child plus another child plus another child plus
another child plus another child plus another child plus another child plus
another child plus another child plus another child plus another child plus
another child plus another child plus another child plus another child plus
another child plus another child plus another child plus another child plus
another child plus another child plus another child plus another child plus

another child plus another child plus another child plus another child plus
another child plus another child plus another child plus another child plus
another child plus another child plus another child plus another child plus
another child plus another child plus another child plus another child plus
another child plus another child plus another child plus another child plus
another child plus another child plus another child plus another child plus
another child plus another child plus another child plus another child plus
another child plus another child plus another child plus another child plus
another child plus another child plus another child plus another child plus
another child plus another child plus another child plus another child plus
another child plus another child plus another child plus another child plus
another child plus another child plus another child plus another child plus
another child plus another child plus another child plus another child plus
another child plus another child plus another child plus another child plus
another child plus another child plus another child plus another child plus
another child plus another child plus another child plus another child plus
another child plus another child plus another child plus another child plus
another child plus another child plus another child plus another child plus
another child plus another child plus another child plus another child plus
another child plus another child plus another child plus another child plus
another child plus another child plus another child plus another child plus
another child plus another child plus another child plus another child plus
another child plus another child plus another child plus another child plus
another child plus another child plus another child plus another child plus
another child plus another child plus another child plus another child plus
another child plus another child plus another child plus another child plus
another child plus another child plus another child plus another child plus
another child plus another child plus another child plus another child plus
another child plus another child plus another child plus another child plus
another child plus another child plus another child plus another child plus
another child plus another child plus another child plus another child plus
another child plus another child plus another child plus another child plus
anothcr child plus anothcr child plus another child plus another child plus
another child plus another child plus another child plus another child plus
another child plus another child plus another child plus another child plus
another child plus another child plus another child plus another child plus
another child plus another child plus another child plus another child plus
another child plus another child plus another child plus another child plus

another child plus another child plus another child plus another child plus
another child plus another child plus another child plus another child plus
another child plus another child plus another child plus another child plus
another child plus another child plus another child plus another child plus
another child plus another child plus another child plus another child plus
another child plus another child plus another child plus another child plus
another child plus another child plus another child plus another child plus
another child plus another child plus another child plus another child plus
another child plus another child plus another child plus another child plus
another child plus another child plus another child plus another child plus
another child plus another child plus another child plus another child plus
another child plus another child plus another child plus another child plus
another child plus another child plus another child plus another child plus
another child plus another child plus another child plus another child plus
another child plus another child plus another child plus another child plus
another child plus another child plus another child plus another child plus
another child plus another child plus another child plus another child plus
another child plus another child plus another child plus another child plus
another child plus another child plus another child plus another child plus
another child plus another child plus another child plus another child plus
another child plus another child plus another child plus another child plus
another child plus another child plus another child plus another child plus
another child plus another child plus another child plus another child plus
another child plus another child plus another child plus another child plus
another child plus another child plus another child plus another child plus
another child plus another child plus another child plus another child plus
another child plus another child plus another child plus another child plus
another child plus another child plus another child plus another child plus
another child plus another child plus another child plus another child plus
another child plus another child plus another child plus another child plus
another child plus another child plus another child plus another child plus
another child plus another child plus another child plus another child plus
another child plus another child plus another child plus another child plus
another child plus another child plus another child plus another child plus
another child plus another child plus another child plus another child plus
another child plus another child plus another child plus another child plus
another child plus another child plus another child plus another child plus

another child plus another child plus another child plus another child plus
another child plus another child plus another child plus another child and

that's killing another child

that's hunting down and killing

another child

a blistering row of children

murdered

and another child

and another child

the children tried to hide

the almighty found them and continued
a child and a child and a child
and 1 more child

count count count
continue counting until the end of your days

another child and another child until infinity
that is what 1 and a half million
         murdered children
             represent

with the approval of a higher power
and with the blessing of god
with the help of and by order of
the almighty

1,000 pages
1,000 books with names
hundreds of names
thousands of names
tens of thousands of names
hundreds of thousands of names and little faces
1 million 5 hundred thousand names
each name is a child   a face
killed
murdered

individually
1 by 1 by 1 by 1 by 1
and another 1
'til infinity
those are your statistics

god allowed them to be thrown in the wagons
god allowed them to be beaten to death
to be burned to death

to be suffocated to death
to be gassed to death

allowed it
and not only allowed it

since god is occupied with every one of us
god was in every wagon and in every train to Auschwitz

god watched
        when the children were pushed into the wagons
watched
        when the doors were shut
watched
        the zyklon b gas do its job

then went to the beach to rest
because even for god
this was difficult
it was a lot
it was too much
and then god returned with another train

I can't believe in this kind of god
because
if this god exists
I'll ask the same questions the priest asked
at Julie and Melissa's funeral*
        'were all our prayers in vain?
        our offerings?
        is god deaf?'

who am I
a speck of dust
in our beautiful universe
to think

---

* In 1995, eight-year-old classmates Julie Lejeune and Melissa Russo were kidnapped in Belgium. They were imprisoned, abused, and starved to death by their kidnapper.—Trans

god is watching over me?

a god who after creation says
'now it's your turn'
that god I can live with

I survived

the people who say
'god exists because I'm alive
I returned from that place'
insult all of those who are dead

I consider this is an unacceptable affront
I tell them
'who are you?
god saved you?
and what did he do with the others?'

that's my belief
it's grown over time

belief

I returned to Auschwitz-Birkenau later in life
on the flight back
a man told me his mother returned from the camps
with strengthened belief
his father too
I'm not criticizing them for believing
but if I say 'I believe in god
because god let me return from the camps'
        I insult those who didn't

all of them

you may well believe after the camps
but not just because god let you live
1,000 coincidences enabled you survive
luck circumstance timing
when possible you could nudge an outcome
I tried to do so and
at times was able to

but many people who were better than me
I repeat
the children
are no longer here

if I were to say
'god let me survive'
why would god have chosen me?
to give testimonies in schools?

no
really
I can't say that

my friend Jacob Cappi Fischler
put it like this
'it can never be said enough
that my parents

our parents
died over and over

they died of sorrow
of loss
because they couldn't predict
what was to come

they died of fear
for what could happen to their children

they died of dread
a terrible dread
of not being able to survive
of not seeing their loved ones again

they died of shame
their forced nakedness

they died
from fatigue
of exhaustion

they died an awful death
because they were murdered for their identity
because they were Jewish

and because we are and will remain Jewish
I ask myself
— without aiming to hurt anyone —
justified or not:
and the ultimate judge in all of this?
is he also dead?'

return to Auschwitz

during the war a cousin of mine lived in the Soviet Union
he was vice president of the navy
he'd changed his name to Bielski
after the war he came to the World's Fair in Brussels
he contacted us and introduced himself with his real name
Klagsbald
later he asked his prime minister to invite me
to the inauguration of a monument in Birkenau
the prime minister had also been at Auschwitz
1967 was the first time I returned
it was like the release of a breath held long and tight
like an expectation fulfilled
not to mention a promise

some may see the fact that I sometimes return

to that place as a form of self-torture
but that's not it

there lie the ashes
the graves of my father
my mother
my sister
my friends and
hundreds of family members

going back is a form of liberation
I return to a place I've lived
though the word 'lived' can't be used
to describe my time there

I intentionally return
Auschwitz-Birkenau is a part of my life
there is no escaping it
I am covered in it
from the tattoo on my arm
to the memories running over
the camps
like a cloak blurring the rest of life

and actually
since I first arrived there
I have never fully left

11

Mondorf 1997

it's spring

2 crows hover low
black and
glistening like the sun
          above my head
they screech
cries that scratch through the air
and ring loud in the sky

more birds
smaller than the crows
float in circles
they call out to one another
each bird painting a song clear in the sky
they flow into each other
a flap of the wing
a whistle that softens
and calls for stillness
the crows grow quiet
I listen along

it's 6:20 pm
the sun drips down
reddens the sky as it glides away
it stops for a moment
as if listening along to the birds
it glows
and disappears

it's 6:25 pm
dusk settles
full and fresh

the moon is sharp
a sliver up high
the birds trill
they lilt loudly
somewhere a clock strikes
6:30 pm

202

honeyed silence
filled with the rising chants of winged friends
sweeter and sweeter
the bird choir sounds

I'm alone in the park
meet myself here
the birds seem to sing just for me
a reminder
a song of immortality
I hear the voices of those who are no longer alive

we were here
we existed
hear
listen
we are here

there is no grave
there is no solace
the moon glosses in a pond
its water still
the music fills me up
from my chest arms wrists
to the tips of my fingers
inside my toes
I am warm
the birds speak
their song catches my breath
it's 7:00 pm

reluctantly
night arrives
the singing quiets down
souls settle

there is no solace
there is no grave

the first photo

Tobias and cousin Schloïme Klagsbald (*right*), photo taken
at their arrival back in Antwerp on April 29, 1945

father encouraged others

father Mozes Schiff in 1917

mother always looked elegant

mother Rywa Templer in 1920

National Archives of Belgium (NAB), Brussels.

Lunia glittered with energy

sister Lunia Schiff in 1941

she was dedicated to her children

mother with Lunia (*left*) and Tobias

grandparents fulfill an essential role in life

grandmother Esther Klagsbald-Schiff and grandfather Chaim Schiff

[Card — top left]

Date et lieu d'arrestation
Datum en plaats der aanhouding
Sobriquets
Toenamen
Profession
Beroep
Ayants droit
Rechthebbenden
Renseignements postérieurs
Latere inlichtingen

*Se trouvait sur une liste de France
(Documentation de Bruxon)
de 249 Belges arrêtés par les autorités
allemandes et incarcérés dans les prisons
françaises, arrêtée le 13.8.42, et interné
à Bourges. Transmis n° 230 Rap 184
Doc.- France 4. C...*

*Décède à Auschwitz le 1.9.42 cf
R.J. 645
F.D. du 19.9.52
Tribunal 1re instance de Anvers
A.C. de Berchem*

[Card — top right]

N° Dossier / Nr. Dossier — 66484 — Catégorie / Categorie — F V

Nom / Naam — **TEMPLER**
Prénoms / Voornamen — *Syma* — Sexe / Geslacht
Date et lieu de naissance / Datum en plaats van geboorte — *Turnow 14-9-02* — *1902*
Nationalité / Nationaliteit — *Polonaise* — *57*
Noms d'emprunt / Aangenomen namen
Adresse / Adres — *Uitbreiding* — Localité / Localiteit — *Berchem* — *11003*
Derniers renseignements de / Laatste inlichtingen uit
Le / Den — *1940* — *1940*

N° matricule / Stamnummer
Par / Door
Décès annoncé par / Overlijden gemeld door
Preuves éventuelles / Gebeurlijke bewijzen
Mutations: camps, prisons, dates, n°s matricule / Verplaatsingen: kampen, gevangenissen, data, stamn°

Nom et prénom du demandeur / Naam en voornaam van den aanvrager
Adresse / Adres — *de Berchem - Anvers*
Lien de parenté ou autres / Verwantschap of andere banden — Nationalité / Nationaliteit

---

[Card — bottom left]

Toenamen
Profession
Beroep
Ayants droit
Rechthebbenden
Renseignements postérieurs
Latere inlichtingen

Drancy 28/8/42
n° 7999

*A été détenu à BOURGES & ORLEANS. Française
le 24-8-1942 au camp de PITHIVIERS. A 65-8-42
au Camp de DRANCY - puis en direction d'AUSCHWITZ
par un convoi parti le 28.8.42*
*Source: Attestation délivrée par Ministre des
A.C. et des Vict. de la guerre - Direction, Contentieux,
Transmise par n° de Dolechot
.n°. 73428/184*

*{Transféré le 28.8.42 vers Auschwitz
{Réponse (en demande) du S.I.R.
T- f.366. Rap 429*

[Card — bottom right]

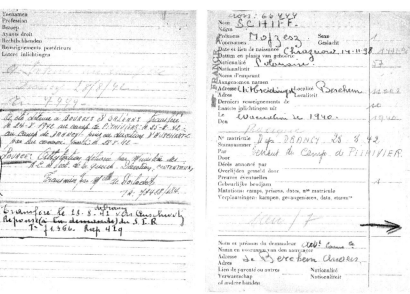

cross: 66444
Nom / Naam — **SCHIFF**
Prénoms / Voornamen — *Mojzesz* — Sexe / Geslacht
Date et lieu de naissance — *Chazanow 14-11-98* — *1498*
Nationalité / Nationaliteit — *Polonaise* — *57*
Noms d'emprunt / Aangenomen namen
Adresse / Adres — *Uitbreiding* — Localité / Localiteit — *Berchem* — *11008*
Derniers renseignements de
Laatste inlichtingen uit
Le / Den — *Waarschijn de 1940* — *1940*

N° matricule / Stamnummer — *Dep. DRANCY 28-8-42*
Par / Door — *Venant du Camp de PITHIVIER*
Décès annoncé par / Overlijden gemeld door
Preuves éventuelles / Gebeurlijke bewijzen
Mutations: camps, prisons, dates, n°s matricule / Verplaatsingen: kampen, gevangenissen, data, stamn°

Nom et prénom du demandeur / Naam en voornaam van den aanvrager
Adresse / Adres — *de Berchem Anvers*
Lien de parenté ou autres / Verwantschap of andere banden — Nationalité / Nationaliteit

official deportation documents of
Lunia
father
mother
and Tobias

Tobias in 1946

Afterword

Transport number 25 of Friday, August 28, 1942, counted one thousand deportees. Among them Tobias Schiff, a seventeen-year-old Jewish boy from Antwerp. On Sunday, April 29, 1945, Tobias made it back to Antwerp. He was one of eight survivors of transport number 25. Eight out of a thousand.

During Tobias's imprisonment, the shame and horror of the century took place, a degrading attack on human dignity. For Tobias, three years of no longer being human.

"Why?" we ask today. Because people thought themselves superior because of their race. This question and answer must continue to inspire us to react against any action and ideology in which people think themselves and their race to be gods.

Those three years shaped Tobias. "I've returned to a place I never left," he writes half a century later in the Auschwitz remembrance book. Tobias has toured Flanders for years. He mainly advocates for acceptance and peace when he speaks to the youth. But also justice.

Reading this book is returning to the core of our existence: the dignity and equality of every human being and the pressing duty to boldly fight for it.

Paula D'Hondt
Belgian Minister of State

Notes

1 My cousin Victor Klagsbald, a cousin of Schloïme Klagsbald whom I mention often in my story, told me during a phone call in 1955 that he lived in Amsterdam with his father and mother during the German invasion. They fled to France and passed through Antwerp. Victor met up with my sister, Lunia. She suggested they meet again the next day around 4:00 pm at the Centraal Station in Antwerp. Victor would come if he could. He was prevented from doing so. They were supposed to meet on Wednesday, July 22, 1942, the day Lunia was arrested during the first raid.

   My cousin talked about this with my daughter Dominique a few years ago. It was she who gently led me to understand what Victor confirmed about that day.

2 This man was mister Baruch Glatt.

3 This man was not sent to the gas chambers and rests in a place where one can visit his grave.

4 I'm obliged to give this friend public recognition. He's now president of the Jewish Museum of Deportation and Resistance in Mechelen.

5 I never saw him again. I learned that he survived Warsaw and was then brought to other camps when the Russian army approached. He was killed by the SS when he ran toward the American soldiers who'd come to free him.

6 In 1993, after the release of my testimony in the film *De laatste getuigen*, I received a phone call from a man who lived in Cannes. This man, Serge Lemberger, told me I didn't have to regret the fact that I had hindered my father's work assignment in Warsaw. He explained that he had been sent there when he was twenty. He said, 'Your father would never have made it out alive. The working conditions were horrific.' That conversation didn't remove the remorse that by choosing to stay together, my father wasn't sent to a camp where there were no gas chambers. But I'm grateful that this man contacted me. Nothing forced him to do that. To showcase the value of this gesture I use the Hebrew expression *Lifnime meshourat hadine*, that is, doing more than what the law requires.

7 In camp language, to 'organize' means to steal, arrange, fix. In short, the word covers everything related to 'figuring it out.'

8   The word 'muzelman' in camp jargon means a prisoner, man or woman, who is at the point of death.

9   Abbreviation for *BUtadien und NAtrium, synthetischer kautschuk.*

10 In his book *If This Is a Man*, Primo Levi also mentions the *prominentenblock*. He refers to it as number 7; however, this is a mistake, as I have been there.

11 I've investigated, this was Bernhard Rakers, born on March 6, 1905, died on August 10, 1980.

12 Ironically, I could say that I knew the English and Americans had disembarked before Hitler did. At that moment, he was sleeping in his bunker. It was forbidden to wake him up.

13 Years later, in 1995, Estelle told me that she wasn't asleep. She'd stayed behind the door and heard everything, especially when I said, 'In Europe, not a single Jewish child is still alive.'

14 For example, when I accompanied our prime minister to Auschwitz on January 14, 1995, he asked me to sign the book for visitor reflections after he'd written the following: 'Never again. The moment some try to repeat history by denying it and nationalism flares up again, this testimony will force us to act so that history shall not repeat itself.' I wrote, 'In the presence of our Prime Minister Jean-Luc Dehaene, I've returned to the place I never left.'

15 A sign that time is passing? A while ago a young woman pointed to my arm and said, 'What happened on 16.02.75?' That indicates forgetting and not knowing the history. That must be fought against.

About the Author

Tobias (Toshek) Schiff (Poland, 1925–Belgium, 1999) was a Belgian Holocaust survivor. Postwar, he channeled his resilience into a career as a diamond broker in Antwerp before venturing into photography with a store in Brussels. In 1989, his journey through the Nazi camps was featured in the documentary *Monsieur S. et Madame V.* Committed to educating future generations and memorializing those who were lost, Schiff dedicated his later years to speaking in schools. *Return to the Place I Never Left* was first published in Flemish in 1997.

About the Translator

Dani James is a native New Yorker, born to a Jewish mother and a Jamaican father, who grew up in Belgium before making her way back home. She holds a BA in English from Baruch College and an MFA in creative writing from the Writer's Foundry at St. Joseph's University.